I0902105

Hiking All Night

Hiking All Night

Poems by Timothy Murphy

Preface by David Mason

North Dakota State University Press
NDSU Dept. 2360, P.O. Box 6050
Fargo, ND 58108-6050
www.ndsupress.org

North Dakota State University Press
NDSU Dept. 2360, P.O. Box 6050
Fargo, ND 58108-6050
www.ndsupress.org

HIKING ALL NIGHT
Poems by Timothy Murphy
Preface by David Mason

Copyright © 2021 North Dakota State University Press
All rights reserved. This book may not be reproduced in whole or in part in any form without permission from the publisher.

First Edition

David Bertolini, Director
Suzzanne Kelley, Publisher
Sarah Beck, Production Assistant
Zachary Vietz, Graduate Assistant in Publishing
Grace Rivard, Publishing Intern

Cover and interior design by Deb Tanner
Cover image: *Moon Shadows*, woodcut by Charles Beck, reprinted here with permission of the Charles Beck family

The publication of *Hiking All Night* is made possible by the generous support of Howard Dahl, Dan Miller, Steve Miller, and donors to the NDSU Press Fund and the NDSU Press Endowment Fund.

International Standard Book Number: 978-1-946163-13-4
Library of Congress Control Number: 2019954160

Printed in the United States of America

Publisher's Cataloging-In-Publication Data
(Prepared by The Donohue Group, Inc.)

Names: Murphy, Timothy, 1951- author. | Mason, David, 1954- writer of supplementary textual content.
Title: Hiking all night : poems / by Timothy Murphy ; preface by David Mason.
Description: First edition. | Fargo, ND : North Dakota State University Press, [2021] | Includes index.
Identifiers: ISBN 9781946163134
Subjects: LCSH: Murphy, Timothy, 1951---Homes and haunts--Poetry. | Murphy, Timothy, 1951---Friends and associates--Poetry. | Outdoor life--Great Plains--Poetry. | Nature--Poetry. | LCGFT: Poetry. | BISAC: POETRY / Subjects & Themes / Nature. | POETRY / Subjects & Themes / Places. | SPORTS & RECREATION / Hiking. | SPORTS & RECREATION / Hunting.
Classification: LCC PS3563.U76195 H55 2021 | DDC 811/.54--dc23

♾ This paper meets the requirements of ANSI/NISO Z39.48-1992 (Permanence of Paper).

i.m. Alan Sullivan

Envoi

Now you are done, go forth my ample book,
            let you give tongue
to each mind-boggling, panoramic look
            we won when young,

trekking on both slopes of the Great Divide,
            Montana or Wyoming.
Each peak achieved, we bedded side by side,
            worn out by roaming.

Breathe with the winds of every sea we sailed
            to our sea grape islands,
confess short fallings at the peaks we failed,
            launched from the highlands.

Far, but not long in time now I shall be
reading Alan this lengthy legacy.

Contents

III. *God Does Not Play Dice*

Preface

It must have been 1990, or slightly later, when I met Tim Murphy and his partner, Alan Sullivan, in Fargo, North Dakota. I was teaching at Moorhead State University across the Red River and found myself serving on a committee with a very strong, dignified Katherine Murphy, whose family had ties to the university. Katherine mentioned that her son was a poet and suggested we meet.

For nearly a decade we met—Tim, Alan, and I, usually in a restaurant for lunch, sometimes at their home south of Fargo on the banks of the river—and talked almost nothing but poetry. Their home was modern and austere, with impressive works of art on the walls and a sort of crow's nest looking over the prairie. Tim was not a hoarder of books and kept only those he most valued on his shelves. Alan, too, was fastidious, exacting in his personality, obsessed with the weather map, which he read with a sailor's scholarship. The two of them could bicker like old hens when their willfulness got the best of them.

On our first meeting I was met with suspicion because I was an academic, and in Tim's mind academics had done much to ruin the climate for poetry in America. He soon discovered that I was a rather odd academic, who felt much the same way about the creative writing industry and the writers it often spawned. He was a formal poet, writing short, pithy lyrics, tightly and precisely rhymed. I too had always felt enormous affection for those traditional techniques, which seemed nearly eradicated from contemporary poetry. We both adored Yeats, Frost, and Hardy, for example, and could quote them from memory.

Working in the family insurance business when not finding capital for companies of his own, isolated from any literary community, Tim assumed he had no allies among contemporary American poets. In fact, he had simply given up reading them. I was able to tell him of a very strong network of writers who shared our affections, including elders like Anthony Hecht, Richard Wilbur, and Donald Justice, as well as poets of our own generation, such as Dana Gioia, Timothy Steele, Emily Grosholz, Dick Davis, Wendy Cope, Charles Martin, and many others. I shared books with him, put him in touch with other writers, and I dare say the conversation changed our writing lives. We widened our circle of friends at the West Chester University poetry conference, held each June in Pennsylvania. Indeed, Tim generously supported the conference whenever he had money to give.

More than anything else, Tim's discovery of the poems of Richard Wilbur, nearly thirty years his senior, galvanized his writing. He and Alan immediately traveled to meet the Wilburs in Key West. As Tim told it, when Dick Wilbur greeted him at the door of his Florida condominium, Tim couldn't help exclaiming, "Mr. Wilbur, you live near the cemetery!" And Wilbur, with characteristic humor, replied, "*Very* near the cemetery, young man." Here was an elder poet who wrote with the formal dexterity of a master, a living figure who could enter Tim's small pantheon of heroes. Tim's loyalty to the Wilburs over the decades was very moving to witness. When I introduced him to my teacher Anthony Hecht, he developed a similar devotion. The first time Tim sent a batch of his poems to Hecht, the older poet replied in a warm letter, having seen instantly the merits in Tim's writing. But he also expressed his shock at Tim's "habits." As Hecht opened the envelope, the pages of poetry he withdrew reeked of bourbon and tobacco.

Readers of Murphy's poetry know he was an alcoholic; the poems are full of confessions, stories, regrets, and pleas for forgiveness. I mention the affliction only because it eventually narrowed the life he and Alan had built for themselves.

When young, they had done much hiking in the Rockies and sailing in the Caribbean. Tim's family were all whip-smart, athletic people who prided themselves on their knowledge of expeditionary feats. They knew all about great yachtsmen and great climbers, while they remained deeply rooted in the enduring communities of the northern plains. Like his powerful father, Vince, Tim was a businessman, but he was also gay, and his sexuality was met with suspicion by many of the people he most wanted to please. He refused to think of himself as an outsider or a victim, insisted on his place in the community that had raised him, and won his place. His business fortunes, however, became erratic due to his drinking. In the first decade of our friendship, Tim made and lost several fortunes. As the years passed, he was less and less able to travel. The beautiful house by the river was sold and, eventually, so too was their sailboat in Florida.

Still, through all of these ups and downs, he cultivated new enthusiasms. The poetry of Australia's A. D. Hope entered his pantheon, and the wonderful New Englander Robert Francis. The little poem he dedicated to Francis is typical of the tight formality of Tim's early work, as well as his enthusiasms:

> Had I known, only known
> when I lived so near,
> I'd have gone, gladly gone
> foregoing my fear
> of the wholly grown
> and the nearly great.
> But I learned alone,
> So I learned too late.

* * *

Friends of mine and I were able to get Tim started publishing books of poetry, and thereafter he produced work at an astonishing rate. One would have to look to figures like Thomas Hardy to find such productivity among modern poets.

I had a front row seat to this productivity for a decade or so, and I was able to see the important role Alan played in the creation of Tim's early work. Tim called Alan "The Editor from Hell"; their editorial sessions often became shouting matches and lovers' spats. Tim honed his talent with Alan's help, and in turn Alan too became a very good poet. They were a team of writers, their partnership culminating in a highly-regarded translation of *Beowulf*.

Readers of *Hiking All Night* will find the productivity of Tim's later years in full throttle. He had returned to the Catholic faith of his childhood, and his faith became a centerpiece of all his writing. My friend Dana Gioia has written about the significance of Timothy Murphy as a devotional poet. The concerns of Tim's early work remain in his later poems as well, often seen with a more forgiving, less jaundiced eye: friendships with farmers, priests, and businessmen in his community; his love of hunting and the generations of his hunting dogs; gay life; his marriage to Alan, always real if not technically legal. The poems take place in a physical world he knew intimately, even as they anticipate a metaphysical finale.

In reading Tim's poetry, one has to engage with his life. He resembles Yeats not only in his tight forms, but also in the way he mines autobiography for his subjects. But where Yeats ultimately constructed a modern political and philosophical universe mightily transcending the self, Tim remains close to home, personal, human and humane, full of genuine contrition and affection for what is near at hand. The later poems are more uneven in quality than the early work, but only because they risk more and range more freely in their meters and subjects. Tim allowed himself a bit of wildness in the late work and gave himself permission to express everything that was in his heart.

This permission might be most movingly exemplified by the final poem in the copious volume you now hold—a private letter to Alan, who died eight years before. Tim missed the Editor from Hell, but also became less constrained by that editorial rigor. He ranges over his most important experiences, ending with genuine regret about his own failings.

> . . . Here I'm mining memories
> from realms you drove me to I'd never seen,
> our switchback trails to tree line's dwarfish trees
> and the dawn's glassy, blue Caribbean sheen,
> the day's first cat's paws, promising our wind.
> Stricken in conscience by one way I sinned,
>
> the crime that I am most penitent of,
> buried in debt and shackled to the plough?
> My failures to articulate my love.
> Let this volume be my repentant vow.

The volume is, of course, much more than repentance. It is prodigious productivity, a life seen finally with more insight than he could earlier muster. It is the work of a remarkable North Dakota poet, a distinctive American voice that even the harsh north wind will not blow away.

—David Mason

I.
Poems for *Hunter's Log*

Spring Bluebills, woodcut by Charles Beck

Early Spring

for Charles Beck

I.

Ice-out, it's only the first week of March.
In early springs our farmlands often parch
for want of snow, but soon rainbows will arch

over our fields, and winter wheat will head,
corn will emerge, the seas of green will spread
to limitless horizons, and each bed

of sunflowers will sport its tiny shoots.
Time for dog training, I grease up my boots
which long to sink into their prairie roots.

Back when I farmed, things were not often so,
excess or dearth, the winters' falling snow.
I pray this is a year when crops will grow

prodigiously, prices our main concern.
For now be grateful for the season's turn.

II.
The Red, only a very minor flood,
the bike path, only a very little mud,
the banks, our pussy willows are in bud.

Soon they will explode in late March pink,
and the stream after its monumental drink?
Back to its banks the vernal spate will sink.

Yet we are still some weeks from roller blades,
riparian woods spreading their leafy shades,
from turning gardens with our rusty spades.

There come some wintry days when I grow gruff,
the snow and ice have lasted long enough,
time for your collar, let me grab your scruff.

Chucky, it's spring and time that we set forth
to patrol the Red River of the North.

What's in a Name?

Unkindness of ravens,
from nesting havens
far to the North
their flocks fly forth
crying Ro-ark,
my mind their mark.

The Great Divide,
two side by side
were cracking nuts
by rip-stop huts.
I knew the crows,
lords of our snows,

but not the raven.
I knew *Godhavn*.

Brother *Hrefn*

Brother *hrefn*,
very often
I fly with you over a blood-stained plain
where wolves and eagles are rending the slain.

Brother *hrefn*,
there's no coffin,
no priest to offer up prayers for the dead
nor words of condolence our Savior said.

Brother *hrefn*,
above us seven
Archangels sing their sonorous laments,
beneath us mangled horses, shredded tents,

and I alight to say Beowulf's Dirge
as in my breast spring tides of sorrow surge.

Uncle Feeney

I still remember, dear,
your nipping Feeney's ear
and dangling from the neck
of my old grizzled wreck,
mostly just skin and bone,
no supple muscle tone
he kept until age ten,
flushing a pheasant hen
or rooster in the wild.
He took you for his child,
his little squirming runt
whom he would teach to hunt
on paths where we had sped.
In two months he was dead.

Fifth Generation, an Ode

Nap Time

Four feet left of my knee
and twelve feet south of his oak,
our baby pin oak tree,
he snores. I sip and smoke.

Our Adirondack chairs
are huge so he can sprawl
twenty feet from the stairs
under our bedroom wall.

Chucky's not hunting birds
because his toes don't twitch;
Murphy is hunting words,
and oh! his trove is rich.

Dream Poem, a Fragment

Winnie crosses my shoulder or my chest.
Missed by a mile on Sunday,
felled for Chucky on Monday,
a gutted pheasant cradles in my vest.

Waking, I could recall the first four lines
and grassy aisles through slender Norway pines.

Fifth Generation

She loved her men, living each day to smooch,
loved Courvoisier, her Very Smooth Old Pooch
as Alan punned. We bred her three years young,
and soon we had an extra raspy tongue
reaming our ears, Dee's noble daughter Maud,
precocious hunter who was never awed
by pheasant cocks, a pointing Labrador
who let my cripples slip until that score
was settled. Now Chucky has brought to five
the generations keeping Tim alive,
long before dawn fast walking for a mile
and scratching ears at sunset with a smile,
every autumn driven through all my gears,
wishing my friend could live for thirty years.

Epode: The Dreamer

I like having you sleep five feet from me,
this morning ribeye with a trace of fennel,
dozing two paces west of my left knee,
safe and snug, curled in your auto kennel.

Your outdoor castle is a grand affair
with sandstone tile in twenty feet of run.
You dream of doves blasted out of the air,
the scent of nitrate from a double gun.

In summer too you sometimes come inside
when the garage reaches eighty degrees,
no climate for a fur coat to abide.
Come in my love, and dream of turning trees.

Li'l Buddy

Last night I dreamed that it was ninety-seven,
and the predicted high was one o one,
Chucky not yet in air-conditioned heaven,
then Steve showed with my reconditioned gun.

This morning it was only sixty-four.
In Phoenix many planes cannot take off
at one fifteen. I'd not go out my door,
let me just drink and smoke and softly cough.

Today is summer solstice. Little friend,
seventy days hence we shall hunt birds
where three counties conjoin, corner and end,
waltzing on wires, realities, absurdities,

as you shake off a lazy summer's sloth
and I pledge St. Michael my hunter's oath.

Poachers

Suspend a pheasant cock
three feet above a brook
on a huge treble hook,
and watch the gators flock.

Poachers won't waste a round
to snuff a reptile's brain.
They thrash in awful pain,
then flop off and are drowned.

Poachers are ancient news,
and some have hearts of gold.
My little brother sold
Dad's alligator shoes.

Never chewed gator meat.
The cocks I poach I eat.

The Fix

Steve has restored my favorite twenty gauge,
an elven smith forging anew my blade,
weapon from youth so treasured as I age,
deadly whether in autumn sun or shade.
One year I bent to fetch a stone-dead cock,
plugged gun in snow, and then both barrels bulged
on the next pheasant flushing from that flock.
When I cased it the damage was divulged.

It shot well, but barrels began to part
five years later, the ribs to separate.
No other gun was so near to my heart,
no harsher judge of any rooster's fate.
Stevie fixed it with some metallic glue
just as bear grease rescues a wounded shoe.

A Second Ode on Parkinson's

for Steve Bodio

To Steve, Eldridge, and Steve

What does it mean to live in Magdalena,
        your eyes on heaven, even
        forgetting you're a Steven?
Are you a frequent wedding guest at Cana?
Parkinson's? I sent you my three-part ode,
cold comfort in adobe, Steve's abode.

Man up! and fix your eyes on South Dakota.
        Come fly a fledgling hawk
        on prairie flecked with rock,
your host a leading brave of the Lakota.
Eldridge Hardie will put you up halfway
but each day's drive a long and grueling day.

Syrdal will come to see a falcon fly
and teach pheasants the harsh facts of the sky.

Letter to Magdalena, NM

Steve, pray to Maria Magdalena
for Parkinson's, paralysis, your pain, a
        short prayer will suffice.

Yours is a disease I fear and hate,
for you come way too early, dreadful fate.
        A romp of nano-mice

run riot and short circuiting the brain
struck three dear friends who spiraled down the drain.
        Alas, it kills you twice,

the day the shakes begin, the day you die
under the deep blue of your desert sky.
        Take courage as you splice

your words together. Pray to St. John Paul.
May Magdalena delay your Maker's call.

Hope is Our Word for *Elpis*

Stephen is taking Gila monster venom
to treat the brain disease I deeply hate.
I pray this treatment hasn't come too late.
Now he can ride his horse in faded denim,
hawk on his fist, young of the year spring kite
as the rose-fingered dawn rolls back the night.

Parkinson's has taken too many friends
as I have written you too many times,
grappling with meters and my anguished rhymes.
The greatest of these pitiable ends?
My pope who strode the world like a colossus
as Homer's longest stiche, the molossus,

leaves its huge footprint in his epic verses.
Jesus, relieve us of our lethal curses.

Parkinson's, Poem Seven

Stone-deaf, Ed said, "I didn't hear you shoot,"
when Dee tackled a cripple in tall weeds
and fetched him to my high-top Red Wing boot,
black-eyed Susans sowing their season's seeds.

Kelly and I drove up to tour Ed's land,
two sections side by side of Beardon loam,
the asking price way more than we had planned,
so far beyond us that we headed home.

Ed's dividends from steel were lowball yields,
but no big spender, he got by on them.
Rich were the cash rents from his fertile fields,
he loved to watch me graft an apple stem,

prompt in paying the yearly orchard bill.
Held in my arms, Eddie signed his last will,
a scraggly X. Memory haunts me still.

For Love of Lead

The love of lead:
affliction that will leave me
when I am dead
and pheasants flock to grieve me—

no, celebrate
my absence from the planet
and defecate
upon my grave of granite,

Goddammit,
into my right hand barrel
a shell: I slam it,
for my inveterate quarrel

with pheasants must march on.
Wake me way before dawn.

Prey

I set my dive planes down thirty degrees
to sink my sub under the stormy seas
and land my bottom with a gentle kiss
a thousand feet below in the abyss,
shut down my screws, my engine. A destroyer
steams over me, depth charges, dread deployer,
but we are running on our batteries,
silent to sonar on a sea mount's knees.

To hunt enter the mindset of your prey
gifted by God and wilier than they
who chase you in the waving prairie grass
and miss you as the dogs and gunners pass.
Seventy yards is all a shotgun's span,
and you are cannier by far than man.

Streeter, ND, 2000

A hundred yards, far my longest retrieve
on doves, a sailor too tough to believe.
Feeney too small to make so long a mark
in the tall prairie, no walk in the park.
I throw my puppy over three-strand barbed wire,
a memory of which I'll never tire,
stride to the spot where Feeney works the grass
and dying flowers where I so often pass
the day before grouse opener. Ten yards,
he buttons it, playing his puppy cards,
then bears it proudly through the tangled weeds,
primaries ruffled, and it scarcely bleeds.
Our second weekend, Feeney's fiftieth dove,
puppy and I well on our way to love.

L'invitation au voyage

for Bill Carpenter

We'll go to Big Floyd Lake and sail my Wave,
        Hobie of course, a boat
        purposed to stay afloat
however wildly winds and whitecaps rave.

Bring two *Calvados*, ribeyes in the bone,
        and we shall grill outside
        as you, playing Christ's bride,
listen to sins for which I must atone.

William, you and I share so many loves,
        Mary Queen out of Time,
        our meters and our rhyme.
Perhaps this fall Chucky will fetch you doves.

Four noble cognacs on my red wine rack
are calling out, "William, come back, come back!"

Shining Prey

Dad held the flashlight while I popped the coon
        which dropped some twenty feet,
        headshot and it was sweet
under a starlit sky and a new moon.

Nightly he tore up newly planted sod
        hunting for tunneled grubs.
        We saw no racoon cubs.
We had a husky never over-awed,

he was a huge bruiser big as she,
        probably fifty pounds
        making his nightly rounds.
Unlike Katrinka he could climb a tree.

Point-blank shot from my teenage .22.
Our sod was saved. That was a night I grew.

Dream Life

Nothing changes unless you make it change.
No, all is flux, and you
must change, try to make do
as each day dawns however new and strange.

I take my first two books down from a shelf,
and how the work has changed
as far afield I've ranged,
hunting this land as I have changed myself.

For two decades going so drunk to bed
I simply didn't dream
beside a burbling stream,
wake with a woolen hat atop my head,

frost in the grass on a midsummer's eve,
or thirty-something hunt alongside Steve.

Dream Warthog

Last night I flew a Warthog, an A-10
closely supporting troops. My Gatling gun
shredded advancing tanks. Infantrymen
had called me to their aid, and it was fun,
fish in a barrel. 50 caliber rounds
bounced off my armor. I couldn't be shot down
nor could I hear the mortars' whistling sounds,
strafing slow motion over a mud-brick town.

Sure, my airframe was forty-five years old,
but twin jets at my tails were blazing new.
Up-armored, I was a troop killer, cold,
two hundred feet my altitude, my view
that of the hungry harrier that hunts,
a hero to all my embattled grunts.

Justified

Blinding fast on the draw
with his Colt .45
and cowboy hat, John Law
keeps prisoners alive.

"Couldn't hit the water
if I fell out of my boat."
So much for killer slaughter,
shave your cheeks and throat.

Shirtless in his tight jeans,
torso to make me die,
in politics he leans
right. The Kentucky sky

on Raylon and his foe
Boyd Crowder always clears,
lets fall nor rain nor snow.
Laughter prevails, not tears.

Too Much Truck

I.

The Ford 150 Raptor—too much truck
for Tim and little Chuck.
We've always loved our compact Ford Escapes,
though often oil pan scrapes
on field road crowns have caused us deep concern.
Drive cautiously and learn
we've not the clearance of my Bronco IIs,
yesteryear's small truck news.
The Raptor? Bring a ladder for the cab,
great room for belly flab
which I don't have, nor have I ample muscle
for our October six-leg pheasant hustle.

II.

Ford on the road,
Chucky and I really not much of a load,
gun weighs six pounds,
bird shot, a case, two hundred fifty rounds.

Time to sing Burns,
forty miles to the highway's S-shaped turns,
first ray of dawn
in the dim East away from which we're drawn.

Each field we'll know,
hunted in autumn or skied in crusting snow.
Hubert, patron saint of hunters, pray,
laden our game vest on this glorious day.

III.
Day's end, now it's time for the long drive east,
            my canny beast
and I, three gutted pheasants in my vest,
            time for our rest.

I think my little Ford could find its way
            were I to stray,
truing the Sheyenne arrow of my route
            after our shoot.

More than eight hundred times I've made this drive,
            as much alive
as on my mountains or the wild salt sea,
realms for infringing on infinity.

Days of 1967

Beer thirty cents a glass
and the same price for gas,
my life, how did it pass

so swiftly down its track?
Gum five cents a pack,
haircut, block the back,

cute but no stellar looks,
dollar each my books,
a cane pole for my brooks

with a hooked angleworm,
a skateboard, hop the berm
and short the summer's term,

head crammed with Irish song,
I camped all summer long.

Ode to the Sharptails

"If mice is the plural of mouse,
grice is the plural of grouse."
—Alan Sullivan

Strophe: The Flush

Today in windless hush
we forage for a flush,
for a split-second rush,

Tim and his crazed young dog
in not yet lifting fog.
Laboriously I slog.

Coveys should hold. We near,
St. Hubert, still my fear
my twenty gauge will veer

wide of the winging bird,
leaving me look absurd.
Hubert, put in a word

high in your heavenly house,
flush us a flock of grouse.

Antistrophe I: A Kingdom

Deadly my double gun,
three shells, three sharptail grice
Chucky fields in a trice,
treble retriever fun.

Rays of sunlight stipple
patches of unploughed stubble,
first flush is a double,
reload and we've a triple.

So up this hill and down
Sunday morning we stroll,
Chucky thinking, "Let's roll."
I have no cause to frown.

Some days we're simply reaping
a kingdom in our keeping.

Antistrophe II: Chucky's Consolation

Feeney stood stud when he was three and four.
    I watched his puppies train
    in summer sun and rain,
coaching them through a Gun Dog Kennel Door.
    Chucky, you'll never be
    FC or NFC,
no bitch with puppies on her whelping floor
will grant you your great uncle's legacy.

There are worse fates than never getting laid:
    never getting to hunt
    or chosen though the runt
of a litter Lone Willow Kennel made.
    Your sire was NFC
    which you think you should be.
Content yourself with grouse hunting this glade,
and pass Feeney in prairie poetry.

Epode: Chucky's Big Black Friends

Cattle think he's a tiny Angus calf,
        pay no mind to my gun
        but when he barks, they run,
Chucky is so uncowlike, and I laugh.

Horses pay no attention to my dog
        unlike the cows that close
        encircling Chucky's nose.
Grouse in my vest, time for a sip of grog,

time for a long, lazy cigarette,
        then hike back to the truck.
        St. Hubert lent us luck,
and St. Michael wielded his sword to vet

two aspirants who hunt this paradise
baffling so many big brown bovine eyes.

Second Sinfonietta

Late Hatch

Moth, fledge in the grass,
no bigger than a fly,
flex wings for the sky
and in a fortnight pass.

October

Leaves drift on the ground.
High overhead the trees
writhe in a stiff north breeze
that searches all I've found.

Patron Saint

In dream St. Hubert comes
simply to loose the locks
on Chucky's kennel box.
Distant December drums.

Come Holy Ghost

Love and life and light:
let me entwine these three
like vines climbing a tree
in a dream poem tonight.

VSOPs

What's for breakfast, Martel or Courvoisier
        or even Hennessy?
        I keep these noble three
atop my wine rack grouped on a silver tray.

Remy Martin tastes too smoky for me.
        No more garlic pickle
        dipped in a draught of Dickel
which used to get me swinging from a tree,

ape that I am, ape I shall always be,
        the knuckle-dragging kind
        flexing an agile mind
to serve the high calling of poetry.

When autumn comes and time to vet my legs,
let it be sourdough toast, bacon, and eggs.

June

Chucky, you've not picked up a tick this year.
    The season it has passed,
    and I'm not yet aghast
at swollen horrors sucking either ear.

We've no mosquitoes hatching in your yard,
    so heartworm I don't fear.
    To August now we steer,
from now on all your lines and casts are hard,

for you must beeline through the blackened flowers
    to fetch each fallen dove,
    your true September love,
when autumn with its shortening of hours

lengthens your aging master's laggard pace
better to fit the frenzy of the chase.

Address to the Deil

Chucky, you are a spoiled-rotten young lab.
Your four legs and your hips, each is a slab
of muscle clad in a jet-black fur coat.
Come drool into my beer to cool your throat.

Maybe two times a week filet mignon
scraps and six times a day a dry Milk Bone,
lots of walkies and blind rigorous lines,
Camp Wilderness for racing through the pines.

Your amber eyes expressive as my speech,
the wild roosters have little more to teach
their scholar, but old Tim has much to learn.
A hot July, and how two hunters yearn

just like your predecessors years ago
for pterodactyl pheasant tracks in snow.

Forty Days, Who's Counting?

"Aim his head to the East,
and he'd run to Duluth,
such a determined beast."
Stevie nearly spoke truth.

Today we practice lines
so you can fetch my doves
from sunflowers and pines
home to my hunting gloves.

Chucky, you're far too short
to mark most pheasants' fall.
Line by the gun's report,
then break the prairie wall.

Practicing for retrieves?
Wait for the turning leaves.

—22 July, 2017

Chucky Gets Screwed Again

Chucky, we're hunting ducks,
first time in many years.
Sitting so still, it sucks,
cold breeze blinds me to tears.

Offshore your decoy whirls,
wind combs the marsh's grass.
Greenheads, tail feather curls
give us one wheel but pass.

Whatever we kill today
I'll pluck and give to Mom.
Ninety-one years and grey
she'll roast them with aplomb,

but you, beloved beast,
will not attend that feast.

Apology for My Bow

A red squirrel moved into the small hip roof
        aloft my stairs and deck.
        The boards are now a wreck
of walnut shells, sawdust. He'll sleep aloof

from all our nasty blizzards when they blow.
        He will not hibernate
        because he thinks it great
to run with red abandon in the snow.

Today I found much of a bunny skin.
        Hours later it was gone,
        up to his bedroom drawn,
soft as a featherbed to snuggle in.

When I was stupid and my views were narrow
I pinned a red squirrel with a broad-head arrow.

Rewards of Industry

My friend, the small red squirrel
who runs atop my fence,
tail in a lavish curl,
is chittering, and thence

he'll nap on rabbit skin
hidden aloft my stairs.
There lies his walnut bin
to banish wintry cares

and tide him into spring
when he can eat fresh greens
and I shall watch him cling
to bark, the elm that leans

over my landing roof.
Industry? He's your proof.

Tip of My Cap to Bacchylides

Yet Another Season

This fall I shall be pretty good but old
        with only half the strength,
        my stride two thirds the length
of twenty years ago. Into the cold

and drifting leaves Chucky and I shall hunt,
        never to bag the game
        his great uncle could claim,
but he will frisk, my happy jet-black runt.

At five he has inspired as many lines
        as Feeney had at twelve.
        Deep in my gear I delve
the Rem Oil for my gun, and Chucky whines

just as his uncle did so long ago,
lusting to track a crippled cock in snow.

But Who's Counting?

His tear-off calendar now down to six,
Chucky counts off the days. August is cool,
sunrise much delayed in these northern sticks,
        and Friday doves will spool

forth from their roosts, into the wheat stubble,
what very little hasn't yet been ploughed,
and four days straight we two will take much trouble
        filling my license. Cloud,

drizzle will not deter us from our task
September One, leaving well before dawn.
My small brass flask drawn from a whiskey cask?
        Sips will steady me on,

and I shall learn how well an old man shoots
when Chucky fetches feathers to my boots.

Sheldon, ND

Half-dozen doves coo on telephone wire,
	stubble alongside corn.
	This hunter wasn't born
to gratify a chest freezer's desire

but work with Labradors, to stand alert
	half an hour before dawn.
	Seconds are drawing on,
I dig my *Mojodove* into the dirt.

From a tree row mile and a half away
	here flies the fluttering flock.
	Parked on a glacial rock,
camouflaged, shoot before break of day,

double and double! We can't seem to miss,
Chucky and Tim in our September bliss.

O Dark Thirty

The truck is packed,
Chucky is jacked.

The Bond

Through juniper and spruce
we weave in knee-high grass.
Chucky is full of juice,
never a flush, alas.
Empty my bag, we're shunting
west, and we call it hunting.

Song rising in my breast,
bunked in a trailer house,
next week much farther west
we shall hunt sharp-tailed grouse
and doves that we shall scour
from rows of ripe sunflower.

The bond of dog and man
Chucky perfects. I plan.

Sorry, Chucky

Upwind, downwind, or cross,
me? I prefer the third,
for how I loathe the loss
if Chucky busts a bird
upwind at fifty yards.
Fingers in trigger guards

simply can't flex that fast.
In dog years thirty-five,
Chucky is built to last,
but I'm past sixty-five,
and downwind we can pass
cocks in the waist-high grass.

No eighty rooster year
    for you, my dear.

Play When Injured

Last weekend Jetty tangled with coiled barbed wire,
so now a blaze orange vest
protects her raven chest
while she bounds madly through the grass, desire
to flush and fetch even one pheasant cock,
as through the grass we walk.

Chucky's never been injured, merely skunked
under a spreading spruce
one day when he raced loose.
This year my faith in pheasants is debunked
by the slow pace of harvesting our corn,
the few birds that were born,

our crowing count down sixty percent,
oh paucity to which we poor assent.

Chucky Speaks

It's a fine life being Tim Murphy's dog.
By his right knee I jog
wearing no leash but my Tritronics collar
as distant children holler
and loudly laughing call
beside a red brick wall.
How I would love to chase their tennis ball.

Kennel and run are big enough for two,
plexiglass for my view,
and twice a day there I am fed and watered.
The wild roosters we've slaughtered
I fetch to stuff my scrawny master's vest
and drool when he filets a pheasant breast.
Now time to curl and rest.

Tim and Chucky Speak

Wrestling weight, every old gay guy's dream,
now when I make my rounds
shirt tucked, my trousers seem
vast for I weigh one hundred twenty pounds.

The Tramadol suppresses appetite,
but my torn shoulder begs
for painkiller. By night
I'm hunting on my sturdy youthful legs

behind a friend three or four dogs ago,
hunting my former farms
in falling leaves or snow
or teasing out fresh couplets for their charms.

I can't recall my seven litter mates,
the first run that I leapt in,
the whelping box I slept in,
our tiny paws scratching at their latched gates.

First memory is my first mourning dove;
for Tim wing shooting is his proof of love.

The Hunter, the Alert Man

Sunlight silver off of a barrel's bluing,
stock swung to my shoulder, instantly truing
bead on the bird by muscle memory,
the crimson fiend flushing from his low tree,
one loud report and Chucky's sure retrieve,
as I believe in God so I believe
in Labradors and my wing shooting. Miss?
Certainly, but days afield are bliss
I would not swap for opera or art.
Mark Chucky's tail, nose down, be still my heart,
legs, you have forty paces yet to spurt,
brain, be Ortega y Gasset alert.

I Think, Therefore Iamb

I am a blue-winged teal
eyeing a dugout pond
with sunflowers beyond.
I cup one wing to wheel.

I am a pheasant cock
guarding a brood of hens,
Lord of the fields and fens.
I mount my crowing rock.

I am a mourning dove
dreaming of Mexico,
flying before the snow.
I was a lad in love,

now just an aging man
recalling all I can.

Too Soon Blown South

No doves, not even at the sunflower plant,
bank of the Maple. Chucky didn't pant,
mouth fouled with feathers, fetching to my knee.
We'll wait two weeks, seeming eternity,
for the arrival of the great migration
from Canada, vast, sparsely-peopled nation
which in youth I so thoroughly explored.
Our locals flapped their little wings and soared
southward in August, borne on a stiff north gale.
On chisel ploughed wheat fields they all turned tail.
We have no stubble on September First
to make their tiny hearts and gullets burst,
Dakota mostly corn and soybeans now,
our combines too soon followed by the plough.

To Richard Arness, M.D.

I don't eat much, but I serenely sleep,
few nightmares and verses that come run deep.

I'm fourteen pounds under my wrestling weight,
two inches shorter, towering not my fate.

Posture is awful, curvature of the spine.
I much prefer bourbon to Bordeaux wine

and suffer from a constant low-grade pain,
my back, but it doesn't afflict my brain.

The eczema is now in its third year,
but UV and the drugs are always near.

My chief blessing? I've energy to work
at an old calling which I seldom shirk.

Of course I'm smoking, drinking way too much,
but this fall I shall hunt without a crutch.

Eight Hunting Sonnets

Bound for Beulah

West of Missouri I went hunting grouse
and passed a D10 bigger than my house,
shovel and digger hauled on two lowboys,
tractor another. I thought "Whoa! cowboys,"
a Cat to dig and pile Dakota coal.
To pass, my Bronco did its shoulder roll,
pilot cars flashing, blocking the Interstate.
The concrete cringed beneath the massive weight.
Twenty miles later rolled a Terex truck,
and then another, traffic backed up, worse luck,
upgraded railway parallel my road,
new coal cars banged together for the load.
Minneapolis needed our coalfield power,
and I knew that my grouse could wait an hour.

September 9th

Borne here by bison scats
grow silverberry and buffalo berry,
ringing this gravel quarry on the prairie.
I hunt the upland flats,

sidehills of the valley
too steep to hazard bird bone, aching ankles.
The deep tear in my right trapezius rankles
on my first sally,

two thousand seventeen.
The flock first spotted thirty years ago
winging back from the river, early snow,
survives, the grouse I'll clean

owed to the young eyes that I boasted then,
the pilgrimage I undertake again.

Slow and Slower

I find that there is much to be said for quiet,
sitting at home, re-reading Thomas Wyatt,
I find I have no further taste for travel
past Ransom County's graded roads of gravel.
Lord, keep me safe, far from a judge's gavel.

I think that someone much younger than I
should float my blocks in bogs. Let him espy
sunrise under the red rage of a sky,
each decoy swimming on its five-foot tether.
I no longer pray for inclement weather.

I care not much if never another bird
falls to my gun, feathers my young dog's mouth.
Come hail, come flood, blizzard or summer drouth
I think *In the Beginning Was the Word.*

Caveant Lepusculi

Our young bunnies are dodging fast and thick,
and Chucky wants to see the pavement slick
with rabbit blood throughout our neighborhood,
thinking, "I'll bet a bunny would taste good!"
in the split second when he breaks and streaks,
and terrified the lucky bunny squeaks
under a fence. The lone dog of my five
agile enough to run them down alive
briefly, after one head shake they are dead,
never to hop home to a tunneled bed.
Strangely, though, he ignores them in the wild
where Chucky wants his master's roosters piled
gutted and fragrant in my little truck.
I bring the gun, and Chucky brings the luck.

Run, Rabbit, Run!

Chucky chased down his fifth bunny tonight,
Hannah running him, wouldn't let it go,
carried it proudly five miles through the snow.
He pulled this trick on me in sunrise light

down by the bike path of the lazy Red.
It was barely a month-old leveret,
the squeal of pain, Murphy can hear it yet,
thumb twist, little *Lepusculus* was dead,

thrown in the river, bound for Hudson's Bay.
Frost's *limitless trait in the hearts of men?*
What about dogs? He collars up again
to ride forth for his pheasant hunt today

with last night's hunting memory to save.
You'd think Chucky sleeps in a fire lit cave.

Careless at Last

I don't worry. Peter at Heaven's Gate
        doesn't intimidate
Murphy, for I'll recite a hunting poem
        and then have leave to roam
with born-again dogs the Elysian fields
until the Dark Lord desperately yields.

My place in Heaven, no longer cause for worry,
        but Holy Ghost don't hurry
to call me from the realm where I was born
        for love of tasseling corn
and autumn with its grouse and pheasant shoots.
Spirit, don't tear your poet from his roots.

Grant me a quarter century, ripe years
to hunt with my old friends and rack our spears.

Lots of Predators

Lion hunting, I can't see it for me,
standing the charge armed with a shield and spear,
red hair straight up, be still my knocking knee.
In our hunting I've just the cold to fear.
Nor would I like to see my Chucky tree
a leopard or hazard the razor tusk
of a wild boar in Kruger Park at dusk.

He is not fast enough for antelope
or springbok, not even for white-tailed deer.
He would give chase, but there would be no hope,
Chuck is no cheetah, that to me is clear.

David slew wolves swinging his shepherd's sling.
All know the end, David becomes a king.

Three Loves in Autumn

Had I a thousand years to live, I would
devote them to the study of the I Ching.
–Confucius

Vermont's hillsides are clad in maples,
farmsteads in Chapman's apples,
cheddar and milk are staples,
and September sunshine dapples
yellow and russet maples.

Wind curries Dakota grasses
like flowing manes, and it amazes
the tourist who briskly passes
a tall shelterbelt that blazes
briefly above the grasses.

Golden aspens on a mountain slope
illumine the Front Range.
In deep dream I often grope
to understand how change
is requisite to hope.

Zaniest Retrieve Ever

We saw no omen like a circling eagle,
        but in the Slough from Hell
        Deezer retrieved a beagle,
a tiny puppy with a tinkling bell.

I stuffed it in the game bag of my vest:
        a pro at carrying young,
        what a retrieving test,
for thirty years a story to be sung.

Phone number, thank God, on its collar tag:
        seems it had chased a deer
        to wind up in my bag,
the guilty owner's conscience scarcely clear,

a five month beagle in a cattail slough?
He was one cringing kid when I got through.

Three Mile Sonnet, an Ode

Thanksgiving Morning

The sere end of the year:
how we love hunting here,
Chucky the dog and I,
where tattered cattails spear
our leaden prairie sky.

At dawn the wind rolls cold
over each pasture fold
of High Plains to our west,
Chucky as always bold,
knowing this is a test

of dog and man and gun.
Today we'll see no sun
for the wind smells of snow
burying Chucky's run
in an Alberta blow.

Blind Luck

My golden BB hit him in the head,
blew *both* eyes through his skull and dropped him dead.
Short grass, so lucky Chucky marked the fall,
snarfed him in seconds (Chucky doesn't crawl),
surely the swiftest of my five black labs
though I have no stopwatch for keeping tabs.
It was a long shot for my Twenty-eight,
blind luck, death I only ascribe to fate.
Young of the year, scarcely a rooster tail,
tops of his wings just turning silver pale,
scarcely a spur, but that means tender meat,
and this Sunday I know what I shall eat,
sautéed breast meat in garlic mushroom soup
with wild rice, truly stew, and I shall scoop
bowl after bowlful from my slow crock pot
and dream of pheasant hunting like as not.

Second-Best Retrieve Ever

Some sixty yards downwind the cackling bird
crashed like a falling slate,
far for my Twenty-eight,
my lucky second shot, I had no third.

Twice hayed, the switchback grass had grown calf-high.
The cock tunneled four times,
Chucky went nuts, and rhymes
started to chime under the windy sky.

Air Labrador the bird tried on my dog,
leaping about five feet,
trick he would not repeat
as I sat smoking on a sawn-off log.

I hit the wing tip, not the shoulder joint,
no chance that he'd bleed out
in grass not dried by drought,
a rooster for St. Hubert to anoint.

I wished that you were there to witness, Steve,
a four sip and two cigarette retrieve.

Three Mile Sonnet

Justice: I mete it out to wily pheasants
over the course of cold, arduous walks.
The law decrees I only harvest cocks,
Chucky, of course, always my leading presence.

Why do I think slaughtering pheasants just?
They taste so good, so keep your store-bought chickens
far from my stove where garlic gravy thickens.
Pheasants and Chucky both will soon be dust

as will this gunner, consumed in gratitude
to spend so many decades in the hunt,
studying litters to select a runt
and field it in this far north latitude.

Much more than a decade they cannot live.
Their gratitude Labradors hunt to give.

Road Kill

Ditch chicken slain by Tommy, my .410?
Nah! Murphy never road hunts anymore.
I need to hear a flushing rooster roar
point-blank out of its frosty cattail fen.
No dog work? Killing isn't even sport
without Chucky flagging his otter tail
straight up seconds before his roosters sail
and drop dead to our Winnie's barked report.

Chucky's Double

The leading rooster plummeted stone dead.
After the bleeding runner Chucky sped

in the tall grass. Close by the one I'd killed
I smoked for five minutes, mortally chilled.

I'd never even seen Chucky ignore
dead bird to chase a cripple to the shore

of a small slough, then fetch his precious token,
bled out, born in his jaws, the right wing broken.

Then Chucky's gimme at the first bird drop
and we had harvested our pheasant crop.

Back at the truck I gutted out the birds,
fresh pheasant hearts for treats and grateful words.

Tim and Chucky hunted in silver fog,
Tim the unworthy master of his dog.

i.m. Governor Ralph Herseth

Strophe: Herseth Ranch

Twenty-five years I've hunted down at Lars
Herseth's capacious slice of paradise.
        In dreams his fields I parse,
and there dream pheasants flush before my eyes.

He farms the east shore of the great Sand Lake
National Refuge where migrating geese
        done with their year's increase
        scream, and his pheasants take
in corn and sorghum plots a long lunch break
        or keep watch in the trees
where I have offered thanks on creaking knees.

First time I'm headed there in five long years
from leafless tree rows, birdless cattail bogs
back home, memories of four ardent dogs
leaving me just six whiskers short of tears.

Antistrophe: Mighty Fancy Shooting

Eleven birds, twelve shells, one cock a double,
hunting in pigweed, not in golden stubble,
        ten minutes we were done,
        two young Labs on the run,
finding one cripple never so much trouble,
        never had so much fun.

Two birds to the hired man to make us legal,
over us soared a hunter, lordly eagle,
        black wings and white head regal,
scanning great rafts of mallards and snow geese
        clamoring without cease,
and every lamb sporting its wintry fleece,

        Jimmy and Lars and I
laughing under the South Dakota sky.

Epode: Homing to Houghton

First pheasant at the South Dakota line,
        a fine, welcoming sign
        to greet the morning sun:
unlicensed yet, I let the rascal run.

Brown County, legal shooting time is ten.
        St. Hubert, please no hen
        colorblind though I be,
but flush a cock pheasant from every tree.

I scout the food plots, cottonwoods in rows.
        Brazen, a rooster crows.
        Murphy, the truck, and Chucky,
St. Michael grant the three of us get lucky.

I am thrice blessed to hunt here once again
recalling all I've lost, both dogs and men.

Return to the Rosebud, an Ode

Ring Thunder Road

Four eagles carve the carcass of a cow.
Hunting is such hard work that scavenging
is a sweet option when you're ravaging
this short grass prairie, virgin to the plough.

Healthy cattle are grazing everywhere
oblivious to their comrade near this road,
its cause of death? Likely an overload
of snow, the North forcing its polar air.

For me hunting is just impassioned sport
but eagles, a matter of death or life.
Talons are scimitars, the beak a knife.
They wheel above us where the gods hold court,

able to spy a cock quailing in grass
where hunted, hunter, rooster, and eagle pass.

Chinook

When a Chinook wind blows
down from the Black Hills' knees,
it warms twenty degrees
and melts the prairie snows.

Badlands bask in the sun,
and blue jays' hearts are lifted
where Cedar Butte lay drifted.
I go with dog and gun,

winded but wintry warm,
walking the draws and creeks
a pheasant hunter seeks
on my friend Huber's farm.

Fargo lies deep in snow,
freezing or far below.

White River Crossing

Rain on the just and the unjust.
—Matthew 5:45

On the south-facing slopes
so infernally dry
the yuccas spear the sky,
and all the righteous hopes
of ranchers are in vain
for a grass-growing rain.

To the north-facing slopes
cling juniper and spruce.
Huge as a six-month moose
a twelve-point mule deer lopes
through the riparian wood,
and God sees it is good,

two worlds four miles apart
where I just left my heart.

Double, No Winchester Super X

Tracking the Cocks

Syrdal and I are dangerous and armed
for cock pheasants, Chucky and Jetty too.
The elite, condescending, coastal view
values us lower than the land I farmed.

Such people think their food comes from a store,
shrink-wrapped or packaged, never turned a wheel
in slick black ploughing, leashed a Lab at heel,
hunting a sport that most of them deplore.

Call me the redneck redhead out of Yale.
In autumn I subsist on what I shoot
and rub bear grease into each Redwing boot.
I live to spare our hens and see them sail.

Schwab Paradise? Two days from now we'll go.
Grant us an inch of newly-fallen snow.

The School of Hunting

I can't recall ten days with so much wind,
four of them gusts to fifty miles an hour,
hunted and drove a thousand miles. Their power
floored me, and I said Lord how have I sinned?

I am a slender target for a gale
and Chucky smaller, sixty-seven pounds.
Lost his first pheasant Friday on our rounds,
long shot, dead drop, certainly didn't flail.

Blood scent? Instantly it was blown away,
heavy cover, worked it a good long while
but no retrieve to make a gunner smile.
Sunday I pray the winds will grant a stay,

a damp zephyr with hoar frost in the grass.
Chucky will ace another college class.

Three Days in December, an Ode

Saturday

My last three days afield
            I have not
            fired a shot.
Today a rooster peeled
out of a favorite spot
but far beyond my range.
I laughed for luck to change.

This morning's overcast
            blew away,
            glorious day,
December halfway past
after a week of grey.
Still right side of the sod
I've paid a debt to God.

Day of Rest

Dreaming of pheasant cocks
I snored with a broad smile,
Saturday six short walks,
none more than half a mile.

I'd limped to bed at eight.
Gunfire commenced at three
in my somnolent state;
a Russian olive tree

upwind and to my left
summoned Chucky and me.
Winnie has little heft,
we were footloose and free

to follow a wild hunch
fit for a Sunday brunch.

Monday

Chucky, we try again
after three epic fails,
flushing a flustered hen.
Off to the trees she sails.

Sized like a hunting boot,
you cornered your first cock.
I don't care if I shoot,
I'm out for a hard walk.

Steve bags more pheasant meat
over our three month season
than we could ever eat,
so strong it stands to reason

that I fall far behind,
mulling my metered mind.

Mind Swathed in Wool Again

"I never made a shot I didn't take,"
said Wayne Gretzky, Lord of the Hockey Rink.
Just missed a shot, too far I *know*, don't think,
skating off on some frozen boyhood lake
while Chucky quartered just beyond my range,
error I've made for years and cannot change

when I am pondering a five beat line,
a found pentameter, what Gretzky said,
or when a rhyme revolving in my head
takes my attention from this wide tree line.
I walk in wet ploughing, each boot three pounds,
vest pocket heavy with my unspent rounds,

happy that on these hard November walks
I often harvest more than pheasant cocks.

Predator, an Ode

for Sir David Attenborough

Two Hunters

"Five of six leopard hunts end in failure,"
not enough speed on the predator's part.
Put here to be a hunter and a sailor
        I know the wind by heart.
        I learn the leopard's art.

Chucky does best working into the wind,
but birds startle us when we quarter down,
the wiliest rooster in a tussock pinned
        not far from Gwinner town,
        red eye patch near his crown.

Chucky's the hound but I the major cat
padding behind silently in the grass,
        a feather in my hat.
Our prey? After the kill I say alas.

Another Song of the North

Guillemots, murres, and auks
nest on the cliffs, their rocks.
Guillemots, auks and murres,
the wind within me whirrs.
I am a short-eared fox.

I want a nice plump bird
and will not be deterred,
for I weary of voles
scurrying down their holes,
never a snack assured.

I who was wintry white
have turned my summer brown.
Long season, sun all night,
long night will soon shut down.

Predator

I’ve been a whale hunting a shoal of krill,
a hammerhead homing in on his kill,
and once fulfilling a warm water wish
I hovered camouflaged, a lion fish.

I’ve been a lab trotting before my man,
a Scottish thane true to my Chisholm clan,
and in my wintry dreams I’ve been a wolf,
hunting hard for the hare I must engulf.

I’ve never had much sympathy for prey,
maybe when I’m too old to hunt, grown grey,
            I shall relent,
            I shall repent,
but I confess, dear reader or editor,
our Lord designed me as a predator.

Brown Bruins

Bears with two thousand times our sense of scent
can smell salmon approaching out at sea.
At estuary mouths their jubilee
proceeds apace, *Alyeska's* banquet meant
to tide them through the winter, the long sleep
when North Pacific snows are drifting deep.

Our sole defense against these carnivores
is nitrate, lead, and the long-barreled gun.
Puny the man who squinting at the sun
vies with his slender fly rod on these shores.
The biggest bear on earth, the Kodiak,
each is a masterpiece, a maniac

in the wild king and sockeye salmon run.
I fished with one, my time was not yet done.

Section Seventeen, an Ode

On a Line from Tom Selleck

I've booted paranoia from my head
over my shooting. Seven birds fell dead,
nine shells, and we had doubled on a pair.
No misses. Farewell, spirits of the air.

Chucky's collar was not cinched tight enough,
so one flushed wild. I roughly grabbed his scruff,
handling the flushes, Stevie, fetch and hold.
The day dawned fair, the morning not so cold

I couldn't shoot bare-handed. Game farm birds,
fast fliers eulogized in ninety words.
Pigweed patches, a perfect proving ground,
you can *save every puppy in the pound.*

Live Training

The *heartbeat of the hunt* is the surprise,
        the flushing cock that flies
        into a storm of lead
        and plummets down stone dead
or swerving soars unscathed into the skies.

At Section Seventeen, a short truck trip,
        we hunt a favorite strip,
        eight birds concealed in grass
        where guns and gun dogs pass,
hoping that not a bird gives us the slip.

Both of our young friends need to work on "hold"
        after their pheasants fold,
        fetch to the outstretched hand.
        Sunday, this dawn is grand,
twenty degrees to make our bird dogs bold.

Return to Section Seventeen

Bearing his braced Wrist Rocket
with buckshot in his pocket
Patrick follows two Labs,
three grownups keeping tabs.
He is not quick enough,
deadly enough to snuff
a rooster from the sky,
but he is *game* to try.
Steve covers when we miss,
four men, two dogs in bliss,
Black-eyed Susan's weeds
sowing their hated seeds.

Windy these short grass rows
but thank God, blowing snows
have yet to scourge the prairie.
Twelve pheasant cocks are wary,
all pretty wild fliers,
Patrick's devout desires.
Two who escape the gun
flee in the Sabbath sun
toward shelterbelts to perch
while four of us skip church.

Three Winters

A bald eagle stayed here for three straight years.
He must have found a freely flowing well
in deep snows of the Sand Hills, and our fell
winters yielded him white-tails and young steers.

He liked to perch a mile from the Sheyenne,
his eyes as yellow as his razor beak,
for fresh roadkill. He hadn't far to seek:
cars raced up Highway 18. Hurried man

did all his hunting for him, lordly bird
choosing rather than migrate to stand fast,
knowing each winter would not be his last
unlike some snowbound yearling in a herd,

his gaze limitless in that leafless wood.
This hunter understood our brotherhood.

A Second Stab at Brotherhood

The osprey doesn't call the eagle brother,
        in fact they hate each other,
eagle stealing the smaller osprey's fishes.
        He could have all he wishes
of upland game or newborn white-tailed deer,
even a freshly castrated small steer.

The osprey plunges in our sapphire lakes
        and masterfully he takes
walleye or northern, any fish he likes.
The eagle must dip talons when he strikes,
for soaking wet he cannot leap aloft.
        Many the hat I've doffed
        walking a northern wood
to the great birds of prey, our brotherhood.

Silver Feathers

How I adore a hoar frost in the trees
        left by a heavy fog
        lifting at dawn, the dog
rarin' to run and I ready to freeze.

Twice I have seen an errant snowy owl
        blown on an arctic blast
        hunched in his shoulders cast
his baleful golden glare at beast and fowl.

Each was an omen for a fruitful hunt,
        three pheasants, sudden luck
        gutted, tucked in my truck,
gifts of a violently polar front:

silver feathers on cattails, trees, and owls
hungrily staring from their hooded cowls.

Dream Stag

I dreamed I hunted with a compound bow
which lets old weaklings draw some sixty pounds,
Stump Lake near Devil's Lake my stalking grounds
where I hunted my snow geese long ago.
Finding the deer trail easy in the snow,
my hunting parka held no rifle rounds,
farther than forty yards was out of bounds.
Under my tree stand, thirty feet below

the does filed by, but antlers were my tag,
I let a spike buck pass, young of the year,
for I was waiting for a trophy stag
and heard snorting before I saw him clear
a hillock on the trail that I'd come down.
I bowed before the twelve points of his crown.

Doubt

Chucky, I had a dreadful dream last night,
seven years on, so I am seventy-four,
you twelve, I cannot help you in your plight.
Dr. Streigel is coming through the door.

Like Feeney at age twelve you are so lame
four landing stairs have grown too much for you,
incontinent, teeth falling out, the same
dog I hunted a decade as you grew

until you so precipitously declined,
more famous than your uncle Feeney now,
your *Hunter's Logs*, new volumes to be signed,
follower of combine and chisel plough.

We lay you on a blanket on the bed,
Beck's Marsh Grasses in blue upon the wall.
I say these verses as I scratch your head,
then comes the swift release of Nembutal.

From puppyhood you strove so hard to win me.
Another pup? I doubt I have it in me.

Return to the Quack Shack

A massive whitetail rack left of the door,
    a Boone and Crockett score (?),
inside hang feathered mounts older than I
    as if making reply:
"This has gone on since hunter-gatherer days
when men first warmed cold cave walls with a blaze."

Wick's grandfather founded this hunting shack
    maybe eighty years back,
and I have been a guest near twenty years.
    We rack our guns, not spears.
Now old, we call ducks from the grey or blue,
doing just what fathers taught us to do.

The Cleaning Shed

"Got enough legs and thighs
to last into next year."
"No way!" Steve Syrdal cries,
"not enough exercise
to last one week this year,"
as he filets a breast,
today a dull knife test.
"Steve, I said *legs and thighs*,
great rhyme," the poet sighs.

Another for Cathy Chandler

Cathy, I'm praying for you every night,
    our shared dysthymia
    (but no arrhythmia!),
the seven decades that occlude our sight.

You've sung high praises for my *Hunter's Logs*,
    never handled guns,
    but all your father's sons
are no strangers to my autumnal slogs,

meat for the table, pheasant, venison
    from snowy field or wood
    where *God saw it was good*,
Sunday dinner a welcomed benison.

The Onset

Let me confess that I pursue my hunting
 way, way beyond reason.
Soon an Alberta Clipper will come fronting,
 snow ending my season,
 bringing the Arctic bunting,
 white flecks beside the road
riding the wind wash of each semi-truck
 bearing its heavy load.
 They winter here, worse luck,
then seek the tundra where they nest each spring,
 snacks for the Arctic fox
 that hunts them in the rocks
after the south gales of the Great Plains bring
clamorous snow geese in their urgent flocks.

Viking Lutheran Church

I often stop in at a country church,
white picket fence and white its slender steeple,
one bell on Sunday to ring in its people.
Here's one whiter than any weeping birch,
its hymnals heaped high on a dusty shelf.
Beside the manger kneels this Nordic elf.

I sing out Holy God we praise Thy name,
        infinite Thy vast domain,
        everlasting is Thy reign,
then *Tantum Ergo*. Here Tim Murphy came
to ask St. Hubert's blessing on the hunt.
We drive into a fierce Alberta front

with gusts exceeding fifty miles per hour
an old hunter confronts with feeble power.

Matthew 5:3–12
Luke 6:20–26

Today we listened to Beatitudes
    where Christ's sermon concludes
warning us of millennia of scorn
    heaped on the yet unborn

who make their firm choices to follow Him.
    However lives grow grim,
we have a shared perception of the truth
    to carry us from youth.

Today we listened to St. Matthew's text,
    but I'll be reading next
St. Luke's mirrors of true virtues and woes,
    thinking about the snows

which will impede me scarcely six months hence
and the two thousand years that lead me thence.

St. Lucy's Day

Strophe

A cock crows in the distance, really lewd,
lusting for hens in spring, for greening grass
and a farm pond pockmarked by breeding bass.
St. Hubert, lately we've been truly screwed.
Team with Michael, head of the Heavenly Host.
For my part I'll recruit the Holy Ghost.

A crimson eye patch and fourteen-inch tail,
white neck ring and red feathers on the breast—
Chucky and I have had a day to rest.
Flush hens for fun, and we will see them sail,
but please three roosters for my hunting vest.
It's three trips since I had a shooting test.

First time this year we hunt Schwab's Paradise;
roosters lie low. When Chucky comes, arise!

Antistrophe I

Dead bird! and *Bird down!* really aren't the same.
Bird down! means Chucky really has to run
nose to the ground, tail high, cock tracking fun.
Wings might be broken but the legs aren't lame.

Today I plan to shoot them in the head.
At twenty yards twelve inches is my lead,
no scent trails where the running roosters bleed,
blows to the brain, and watch them drop down dead.

Ten miles to go, Hubert, let me believe
in Winnie's shooting, sure that pheasant cocks
will flush in range on each of our short walks,
believe that Chucky nails every retrieve.

Last day to work out our bloodthirsty yen,
hope springs eternal, hearts of dogs and men.

Antistrophe II

Three shells, ten minutes, a three rooster hunt,
a one row tree line and a cattail slough,
maybe four hundred yards and we were through,
flushes so close the cleanup man could bunt.

Doctors and lab tests, Thursday and today,
yes, River City has minor trouble,
no more excursions to our snowy stubble,
a major Arctic cold front on its way.

Chucky, no more dog walkers come next spring,
forty minutes for three miles, we'll get on it,
just enough field time to compose a sonnet.
Then come September let the doves take wing

from sunflowers bowing their ripe black heads.
I pray Doc Johnson weans me off my meds.

Epode

I love it when a cock flushes behind me
as he outsmarts the dog.
I whip round in mid-slog
working westward and let the sunrise blind me.

I love it when a cock crows in a tree.
They have such wicked smarts
I think in their black hearts
they have a dire dread of mortality.

I love a breast in black bean garlic sauce
simmering on my stove.
Under the grass he dove,
his wiles for Chucky just a gain, not loss.

I give thanks for the Great Plains we are given,
for hearts by horizontal grandeur riven.

II.

The Mahli Poems

i.m. Maurice Mahli

Proud Father

Closest of friends I wanted for a son,
purloiner of one double-barreled gun,
a BSS my father gave to me
when I was sprouting by his old oak tree.

Well, pass it on to Patrick when he's tall
and old enough to try a belly crawl
on grazing geese. Let's hope he bags a double,
I've never belly crawled, way too much trouble.

Danny, it's fun to teach my young best friend
to load a Stihl weed whacker and to bend
sharp eyes onto the bevel of a knife
and bear some lessons thence into his life,

all while his eyes are glowing blazing blue
as yours decades ago when I met you.

Fourth Pentecost

I.

Daniel Timothy, soon you will start to hunt
just as your brother did four years ago
both in September heat, November snow.
At first you'll be a little soldier grunt,
four strides to my two, but you'll grow tall
in soybeans where the sneaky roosters crawl.

Greetings today on your fourth Pentecost,
the mighty wind followed by tongues of flame,
the gift of tongues to preach our Savior's name,
the Holy Spirit strengthening the lost
apostles gathered in their cheerless room,
a day to mark the turn in human doom.

I hope you'll like this when you're fully grown,
a very first sonnet to call your own.

II.
Think of your big brother,
your father and your mother,
your sisters whom you smother

with kisses or tiny blows,
your rage comes from God knows,
trembling from head to toes.

Come time for breaking hearts
and your namesake departs,
taking with him his arts,

may gratitude's warm glow
however deep the snow
go with you where you go.

Then there's the wild blond mop.
May curls you rarely crop
hop wherever you hop.

"Dad, this is for Yale."

Blue eyes under his honey
colored curls, Patrick mows,
brushes bugs from his nose
and gives Danny my money
to fund his distant college
and sate his lust for knowledge.

Patrick has underbid
Remy Bosh for snow.
Come on a cruel blow,
he's such a little kid
Murphy will help him shovel
sidewalks around my hovel,

twenty-some Charlie Becks
textured by chiseled checks.

Another Birthday Boy

I.
I give Patrick a honking huge sheath knife,
a Buck of course, and Kim, mother and wife
will shake her head, a hard Arkansas stone,
two years will pass before he has to hone
its factory edge. No digging in the dirt,
scaring of any girl in her plaid skirt,
serious tool only for cleaning game
or whittling wood. Old Uncle Tim to blame,
basic geometry, thirty degrees
to whet a blade for blazing North Woods trees.
I use saliva, he'll use honing oil,
and he will learn to love the yearly toil
of sharpening his knife, whacking each head
from his first pheasants, making sure they're dead.

II.
Kim once said, "What a happy little redneck."
Saved as I've been from any drunken road wreck,
I plan to see my buddy growing tall,
tall as his father, yellowing ash the wall
shading him. When he was armful small

Ego vos baptizo, decade ago,
an April day swirling baptismal snow,
his twin Elizabeth I also blessed.
Pheasant hens were peering from every nest
they thatched some ninety miles west by southwest.

Where have they gone, these years totaling ten?
How fares this year the wintered pheasant hen?

III.

Next year, Patrick, you're old enough to Scout,
        then Hunter's Safety Course.
        Danny won't have to force
our great outdoors. I've never seen you pout,

not even porting Murphy's heavy gun
        for five long miles last fall.
        Soon you will grow so tall
it will seem pheasant feathers when you run

hot on your little buddy Chucky's trail
        in Chub Schwab's prairie grass
        which I minutely glass.
Lace up your boots. Little you try will fail.

Patrick Mahli, an Ode

Altar Boy Latin

Decimate means kill every tenth man,
harshest of disciplines for Roman legions
fighting in Gallic or Germanic regions,
a punishment for troops that failed and ran

rather than face their foes. So we abuse it,
the Roman word, I mean. Let us restore it,
dishonor cowardice. Let us deplore it,
and the accusative, well, let us use it.

Next year my small friend will be serving Mass
and start his long slog up the Eagle trail.
Bearing my Browning he will never quail
on pheasant drives through chest-high prairie grass.

This year I must rethread a mainsail batten,
my buddy's second year of sailing camp,
next year tenting under a Coleman lamp,
and Patrick Mahli is beginning Latin.

Honorary Grandfather

I'm growing slowly in this sacred role.
I'll never have a grandson of my own,
        flesh of my blood and bone,
a sapling sprouting by my aging bole.

A decade back I baptized little Pat,
Elizabeth his twin, my text was Latin,
        their blankets' fringes satin.
Tim in his tie and pinstripes doffed his hat

while Kim and Dan swore the baptismal vows.
"Do you renounce Satan and all his works?"
        In Pat no evil lurks.
He pushes mightily beneath my boughs

because his first job is to mow my grass,
as tall at ten as I was at eleven,
        hunting his way to Heaven
for wild pheasants that flush and flaring pass.

By Bits and Bitts

Patrick, I'm glad your new jackknife is dull,
    time for your fine-grained stone
    and oil with which you'll hone
a blade to gut the pheasants you will cull.

Poor excuse, this, for a factory edge,
    but stroke it razor fine
    and it will trim a line
when you lie stranded on a mountain ledge

with high aloft your buddy and your packs.
    Tenth birthday close behind
    and pell mell your young mind,
next year I'm giving you a cedar axe.

Someday you'll snub a clove hitch round a bitt,
    your slim sloop sloshing by
    the dock, wild dog the sky,
the gale a test for all your strength and wit.

Four for Patrick

Temp Perdu

I can remember when
I was just turning ten.
You bear me there again.

Topping a deep tap root
I wasn't wildly cute.
In two years you will shoot,

but now I teach each knot,
hoping you'll helm a yacht.
May everything I've taught,

Jack London and Mark Twain,
pitching a tent in rain
guyed for a gust front's strain

stand you in perfect stead
decades after I'm dead.

Lesson XLV

Now you will clean a gun,
Winnie, my favorite one,

time to improve yourself,
take solvent from the shelf,

screw in the copper brush
mounted on rods, don't blush,

ten times down either tube,
next the protective lube

sprayed on a cotton swab
soft as a fledgling squab,

then steel surfaces sprayed
and my dear Winnie laid

into her shearling case,
soon to resume *The Chase*.

Ad Altare Dei

It's time that you serve Mass,
water and wine in glass
cruets, not gold or brass.

Time for the Holy Ghost,
to hear the Heavenly Host,
anchor by Heaven's coast.

Anchor, symbol of Hope
for which we grimly grope
climbing a rocky slope.

Your pastor's robe of satin
fold as you learn your Latin,
feast that will never fatten

become your daily bread,
halo on your blond head.

Testament

Now let me make my will,
bequeath you every kill
and shoulder of a hill

I've hunted, every slough
my decoys swam, their blue
mirrors of glass, a new

Labrador pup to pass
days in our seas of grass,
stubbles of beaten brass,

our ten-row lines of trees,
my infallible knees
plodding under their lees,

my elbow's shotgun crook
and this, your hunting book.

Summer Slide

for Patrick Mahli

The "Summer Slide" doesn't apply to Scouts
learning to camp and cook, to hoist a pack,
basic knots on the Pioneering rack.
Lesser boys were the "ins," we were the "outs."

Mashing up burdock tubers from the woods,
wild berry pancakes, snaring a spring bunny,
learning jokes long in the tooth but funny,
tramping in rain under our sweatshirt hoods,

mastering both lifesaving and first aid,
building a monkey bridge or signal tower,
kneeling in chapel at the sunset hour,
mowing the lawns with which this small boy paid

Wilderness fees starting at age eleven,
we dreamed all winter of our weeks in Heaven.

Little Pioneer

I teach Patrick the seven basic knots.
    Soon he will learn to lash
    a birch bough to an ash,
sign of the cross to elevate his thoughts.

Someday like me he'll build a monkey bridge
    diagonally lashed
    where Scouts in hundreds splashed
under the fragrance of a pine-clad ridge.

I wonder if he'll sew his Eagle rank
    onto a Boy Scout shirt
    soiled with a summer's dirt
and have a kindly Scoutmaster to thank.

Two years from now he'll swing a double gun
and learn new meaning for an old word, fun.

III.
God Does Not Play Dice

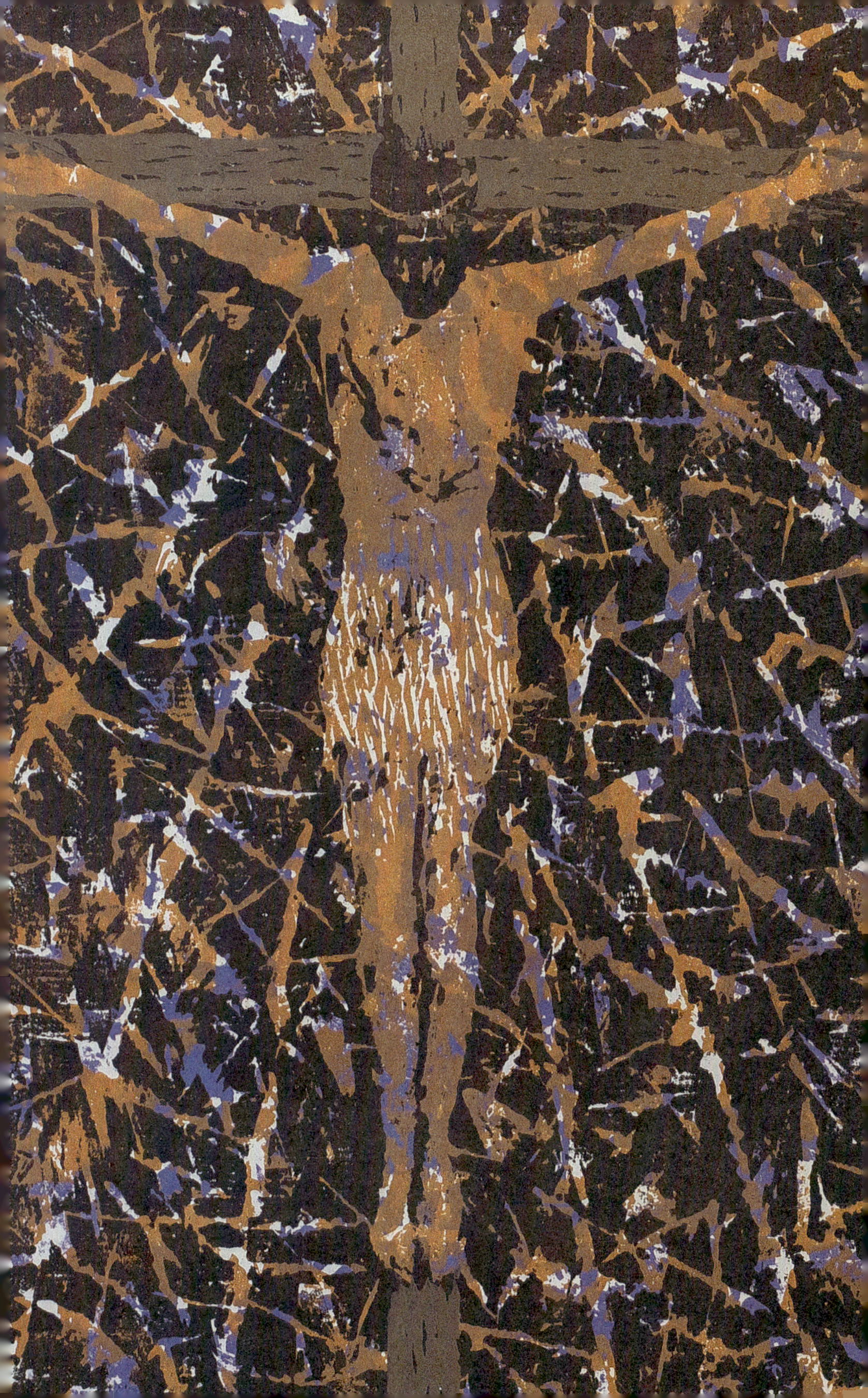

Ecce Homo, woodcut by Charles Beck

God Does Not Play Dice

When grazed the last free-ranging buffalo?
Not long before our last Alberta blow.

When did the grey wolf and the grizzly bear
abandon us? When red men in despair

danced for their ghosts because the whites had won,
no more singing with brandished bow and gun.

When did the creeks last overflow their banks?
Only two years in ten. Kneel and give thanks.

Time passes, friends. We live only a minute
since Robert Burns first praised the lowly linnet

singing her heart out in the blooming heather.
I measure days by changes in the weather.

Time is a fiction, though a stubborn one,
thought he who sought the birth date of the sun.

Address to the Manger

Sleep, infant, sleep
among the oxen and the sheep
which kneel before your manger.
Welcome to danger.

When you become a man
preach us the good news while you can
before you bear the scourge and cross,
an everlasting loss

we all bear to the grave
with guilt. It was your doom to save
us sinners, us ungodly men
whose sins slay you again.

You could have claimed your own
Egypt, a Pharaoh's golden throne.
Instead, as Gabriel blows his horn,
child, you are humbly born.

—2012

To Our Lord on Christmas Day

Rise, infant rise with Your sad eyes
blue as Jerusalem's skies.
Rise from the straw. Someday the Law
will flog Your backside raw.
Flee to the sands where Egypt stands.
Work wood with Your hands,
and grow to teach three years and preach,
engendering in each
ear that hears Your word the once absurd
truths billions have heard
two thousand years since Roman spears
and a crowd's cruel jeers
waited upon Your crucifixion,
Your final benediction.
Many still think it fiction.

—2017

A Reversion

"The poor man's Mass," Tom called the rosary,
harking back to when priests hid underground
and Ireland's money was the British pound.
A child, I counted beads from memory

and haven't said it now for fifty years
but say my three Hail Marys every day,
at night, rather, as I kneel down to pray,
to dream of the centurions with their spears

and Christ gasping "Woman, behold thy son,"
meaning St. John, alone among the twelve
to climb that hill and decades later delve
vision from Revelation. I have run

far in the field and farther in my mind
since I awoke to learn I had been blind.

Poet, Yes

Poet, yes, but mainly Evangelist:
    Evangel, Gospel in Greek,
    and Spirit let me speak
grounded in faith, and please let every tryst

with my Lord's body rejuvenate my fervor
    to wrap verses in rhyme
    and use my remaining time
to praise God as my Savior's faithful server.

Spirit, let me proceed by indirection,
    praising Your montane trees,
    the sweet salt of the seas,
to find in prairie beauty Your reflection.

Gratitude at 4:00 a.m.

Let me write one more time on gratitude.
It is a virtue much like love or hope
brought to vicissitudes with which we cope,
it is an eye-spliced rope, an attitude.

What am I grateful for? That I was born,
that against the stacked odds I'm still alive
well into seven decades, that I thrive
despite my failures practicing French horn,

guitar, piano, turning in my teens
to the intoxicant of metered verse.
It is a gift I cannot reimburse,
not with this steaming bowl of ham and beans,

only with work engaged long before dawn,
the small lantern to which my moth is drawn.

Sonnet at Midnight, an Ode

Prayer for my Sixty-seventh Lent

For forty days churches go largely dark,
    no water in our fonts,
    we cold shoulder our wants
to wait for Easter and the rising lark.

No hallelujahs in the daily Mass,
    our favored sacrament
    Confession. Surely Lent
as for two thousand years will sadly pass.

Then comes the Vigil with its ringing bells,
    the blazing lights in churches,
    archangels on their perches,
the catechumens and the Gospels' spells

to ward the dark off for another year.
Bring Him a sponge of vinegar, a spear.

Prayer for my Sixty-seventh Pentecost

Grow little book, now seventy-seventh page:
        as I age
you are a sovereign cure for all my pains,
        the rusty chains
that weight my legs and slow my blistered feet.
        Lord, I entreat:
support me on my gentle, downhill way,
        bless me each day.

You are the reason I have lived to write
        by dawn or night
maybe five days in seven every week
        a verse to seek
absolution for my manifest wrongs.
        Dictate Your songs.

Sonnet at Midnight

Robins sing me awake at four a.m.,
        another day to work
at the high calling which I seldom shirk,
rhyming, then fall in bed at nine p.m.

This afternoon I napped nearly three hours,
        so midnight I just marked,
and every bird that through this May day larked
is fast asleep, netted in Hypnos's powers.

Twenty some hours I have been up today,
        pecking at little keys,
scratching the eczema that plagues my knees,
breaking only to nap, to eat, and pray.

These lines I augur to a silver bin
to store against the burdens of my sin.

Fire

Fire, not the scorch of a red-hot stove,
        but a beckoning light
calling the weary traveler at night
to a warm cottage in a maple grove.

Fire, yes the flame of a burning bush
        on an Israeli peak
where truth lodges that every soul must seek:
God rules from Fargo to the Hindu Kush.

My favorite fire alights on every head,
        twelve of them in a room
gathered for supper in the gathering gloom,
firmly believing Jesus is not dead,

Gospels to write, a world to hear His name,
unsinged moths round an undying flame.

Righteous Nap

I nap today: Tomb of the Patriarchs.
A smithy smokes beside it. Brilliant sparks
fly from a red-hot blade, a hammered sword
I am to wield for Jesus Christ, my Lord.

An angel plucks me to the Wailing Wall,
high over my right shoulder stands the tall
Dome of the Rock. A muezzin hails the day.
Slipping my shoes off it is time to pray,

crossing in stocking feet the figured tile
with arabesque designs. Does Allah smile
to see a red head on the Temple Mount
milling among His pilgrims beyond count?

Whisked to a stable bedded down with straw,
my head swimming in the Mosaic Law,
I greet three kings traveling from afar,
led by a supernova, blinding star.

Now I am climbing Calvary, a hill
where Christ our Savior is suffering still,
nailed to a cross, a perfect sacrifice,
and every mortal sin murders him twice.

More angel wings, Masada. There I stand,
Jerusalem below, a sea of sand.
So my first voyage to the Holy Land.

Two Nights, Two Dreams

Bedtime Confession

Come Holy Spirit, Creator blest,
And in our hearts take up Thy rest.

Memory loss is what I fear the most.
    Two seizures in my brain
ten years ago with their head-splitting pain
wiped clean my memory. The Holy Ghost

and patient years' mnemonic exercise
    have brought me slowly back
not to my prodigious boyhood track
but back to dream in rhyme and waking rise

holding a text verbatim in my head.
    What other poet's gift
so comes from dreams where we so nightly drift?
Holy Spirit, time that You come to bed.

Acts 2:3

I once was lost but now I'm found,
Was blind but now I see.

Acts of the Apostles,
long since my favorite Book,
reading it I hear throstles,
our ancient name for thrushes,
and how their singing hushes
this kitchen where I cook.

Lost and Pentecost
I have too often rhymed
in summer and in frost
as from my fields I climbed,
a bird whose wings were limed.
I who am found was lost.

Each night a tongue of fire
descends on my red head,
the dreams I so desire
follow me to my bed.
All that runs true and deep
comforts me in my sleep.

My Start

Giant steps on the path, *Paradise Lost*,
six books to learn by heart
in five beat lines its art,
no regrets for the many months they cost.

Blake said that Milton took the Devil's part,
and so surely did I,
through decades I decry,
while always thanking Milton for my start.

So *The Inferno* is the only book
in Dante's masterpiece
declaimed to wheeling geese.
I still give it a long, despairing look.

Five decades I have scaled a winding stair,
only now looking back down in prayer.

Three Gospels

"Take no sandals, and take no moneybag."
"Sell all that you have, and follow me."
"My yoke is easy and my burden light."
So Christ intimidates us from the height
to which he once ascended from His tree,
loving us always, always. Despite the lag
of these two thousand years, He is made new
with every Mass and every sermon preached,
in every verse this lowly servant writes,
so many dreams that sanctify my nights.
Myriad are the Christians he has reached.
My days begin damply in morning dew
for my long drought passed by me, and the rope
to which I cling rhymes perfectly with hope.

Anpiel

The B-V shift? Then call him *Gavriel.*
Please thank him for hauling my ass from Hell,
though likely that was belovèd Anpiel

who silences my frightened childhood screams
and drags me from the dark nights of my dreams,
flexes his wings, exactly as he seems,

my Guardian. He came twelve years ago
sent by the Holy Spirit in the snow,
my finger on the trigger, set to blow

my brains out, spattering my cherished books
on which I'd lavished long and probing looks,
but I was dangling hopeless, Satan's hooks

digging my shoulders where an angel's wing
might sprout were I not such an earthbound thing.

Reformation

Five loaves, two fishes,
basket, no dishes,
this listener wishes

to sit on that hill
and swallow my fill
of gospel until

Christ leaves via boat
so briefly afloat,
his carpenter's coat

untrimmed with ermine.
Read every sermon
in Luther's German.

1517–2017

Tiny Prayer I

Lead me not into temptation,
leave me not to damnation,
but deliver me salvation.

Tiny Prayer II

Forgive me, let me be
nearer, my God, to Thee.

Repent

Men are not angels, so
we swallow all our pride
and beg God to abide
our sinful ways below.
His Son died on a tree
to save both you and me.

Men are not angels, so
for eight weeks we repent,
the dead of winter, Lent.
Then Easter Vigil's glow
lights up each darkened church
where three archangels perch.

In Lent the Prophet starts,
"Rend not thy garments but thy hearts."

Johnny Junior, an Ode

Second Week of May

We walked, the apples nearing their full blooms,
        Mom pushing ninety-one,
        slow, and the midday sun
brought memories to the capacious rooms

our minds accord them when we're growing old.
        The future fades away,
        and who cares for today
when we've so many stories to be told?

Apple-Stuffed Turkey

Dan Mahli and I, tom turkey feather
        gracing my Stetson's brim,
        the rolling clouds were grim,
two of us in for harsh October weather.

"Where did you get *that!*" "Shot him in the trees,
        plucked, smoked, and cooked,
        devoured." That lie is booked,
logged in my store of autumn memories.

Robert o Lincoln

Orchard in bloom, male bobolinks returned
        to lead their dusky hens
        to the subarctic fens
where pairs unite, and all their passion burned,

hatch baby birds. But now atop each tree
        Bobbies o Lincoln trill.
        For thirty years the thrill
of hearing them has held me fast in fee.

Pommeculture

I grafted eighteen types of apple trees,
stout cultivars resistant to disease
whose fruit would knock me to my grateful knees.

Scions and host wood from my sturdiest stock
I notched and married to withstand the shock
of grafting, and the cider in my crock

summoned me home to sample my reward
for making apple saplings for the Lord.

O Holy Night

Two octaves way below young Aled Jones
and one beneath the tenor he became,
they both defeat my upper register,
this soaring song for our great Magister.
I shouldn't sing them my unlovely tones,
my boy soprano hangs his head in shame.

A work of genius is this great duet
between one singer thirty years apart.
Few songs conjoin such longing and such joy,
the man plays like a cello to the boy.
First time I heard it, I was sure I'd met
a human echo of the angels' art.

"The god of that has left me," said my Master.
Hearing two angels? Play them for your pastor.

Church of SS. Anne and Joachim

for Fr. Paul Duchschere

Marvel of marble, walnut pews, stained glass,
nave reaching so *achingly toward Heaven*,
three golden arches quoting Psalm Twenty-seven,
virtues inlaid into its aisle surpass

any church's I've seen around the world,
its ambo where I've served as liturgist,
and when I take our Holy Eucharist,
I'm kissed by Christ, and up my soul is whirled

in a great roar of Pentecostal wind,
Baptistry, choir, its structure cruciform,
its youthful congregation always warm
to an old gay however I have sinned,

Anne and Joachim: in old age they gave birth
to one who bore the Savior of our earth.

—*On their Solemn Feast*

Another Pep Talk

When you're far gone it's far long to come back,
        to greet the Holy Ghost
        and take His proffered host,
carry your cross aloft a stony track.

Open your heart. The Lord will clasp you fast.
        No one is driving nails
        through hands and feet. The sails
of Peter's fishing boat will waft you past

all leeward, iron headlands to a beach
        of black or yellow sand
        depending where you land.
Evangelize, you are put here to teach

the little you have learned in your long life.
Your Savior? Strive to be His worthy wife.

The Protomartyrs

Imagine you are Mark sailing to Rome
        to sit afoot Saints Paul,
        Peter, and transcribe all
the legends that their memories could comb,

or James preaching in far-off northwest Spain
        whose path our pilgrims take
        for Santiago's sake,
a march nearly to Biscayne's breaking main.

Timothy preaching in Byzantium
        was St. Paul's closest friend,
        two letters at the end,
both saints contemplating their kingdom come.

Crucified, stoned, beheaded, all passed on,
great age gifted only to good St. John.

Mark 1:7

"I am unworthy to unloose his sandal,"
  said one who leapt in the womb,
  whose murder is a scandal
two thousand years after he met his doom.

"I only come to baptize you with water,"
  but Herod's daughter
asked that his head be served upon a platter.

First cousins, John the Baptist and our Lord,
  the first to be revered
  but Jesus Christ adored
after our Lord was crucified and speared.

St. John baptized just to make straight the way,
  then Christ taught us to pray
Our Father which I kneel for every day.

Feast of Christ's Baptism

Father, I only seek to please,
not as Your godly Son
but just as anyone
fumbling in darkness tries to find Your keys
which Moses numbered ten.
Each key must deftly open the oiled wards
to free the door that leads us towards
God from the soiled world of men
of which I swiftly tire,
my body breaking down,
eyes fixed on the seven stars in Mary's crown,
Heaven my dear desire.
Think of me as a pup dying to please,
pouncing with little paws against Your knees.

Double Sonnet from Four Verses

Matthew 3:17 and 17:5

This is my Son with whom I am well pleased,
        words spoken by a dove
        bearing the Father's love,
a white wing by the Holy Spirit seized,

first spoken at the baptism with St. John,
        immersion in a river
        for mankind's great forgiver
dipped in the water thrice, who thence passed on,

then said again out of a brilliant cloud
        where James and Peter spied
        Moses at Jesus's side,
before the rolled-back rock and snow-white shroud.

Lord, like that dove may I be truly seized.
This is my Son with whom I am well pleased.

Matthew 9:37 and 24:36

The harvest is rich
and the laborers few.
When I lay bleeding in a ditch
all that I knew
was I needed my Savior's aid.
You do not know the day
You do not know the hour,
then Jesus latched the door.
I am as I was made,
Catholic and gay.
Knowing my Savior's power
I pace my maple floor,
finding new ways to pray
in which I set my store.

Acts 20:7–12

for Father Paul

Eutychos plummeted from the third floor
    of a large Troan hall
    preached in by St. Paul.
Horrified spectators rushed for the door.

He had been seated in a window well,
    but Paul preached for five hours.
    Beyond his boyhood powers
to stay awake, our small Eutychos fell.

This was no nap, no ordinary faint.
    Lifeless lay the youth,
    deaf to our Savior's truth.
It was the first miracle for our saint,

a deep coma with neither pulse nor breath.
He saved a boy so nearly bored to death.

Dream Offering, October 8

Tonight I dreamed I was a crippled Jew
        offering up the strain
        of muscle tears and pain
to G-d who nightly makes our world anew.

Short night, a chronic ailment, right foot cramp:
        I rise and climb my stairs
        to knead out its despairs,
then sit to work beside a yellow lamp.

Lord knows no one has suffered like the Jews
        lo these three thousand years,
        their Lamentations, tears,
so all are trialed when G-d turns the screws.

I love a Jew tortured upon a tree
Who died to set His fellow sufferers free.

Two Miracles

Five loaves, two fishes,
five thousand hungry wishes,
let every soulful camper
bring a big willow hamper
for scraps after his fast.
Save the best wine for last.

Grisha

"Ah yes, I hear Greg is our Great White Hope,"
        which I would never say
        but Wilbur did one day.
I hope Greg showered with a lot of soap.

Memorable, lines married from the tongue
        to a reflective mind
        that leads the halt and blind,
Greg writes more than my friends among the young.

Lines read in drought the year when I went bust,
        often recalled in dream:
        "...The singing of a stream
and that it wore a diamond down to dust."

Aging Ladies

Once more I walk into an empty church
and belt out Holy God We Praise Thy Name
and *Tantum Ergo*. Hymnals you can search
for verse that comes anywhere near the same
to glorify our Lord, to shrive my shame.

Two aging ladies, rosaries, in prayer:
startled to hear my baritone they turn,
near as they are, foot of a winding stair.
In their blear eyes I see my fervor burn,
the unity with Christ for which they yearn,

the purity which I may yet achieve
when I am readying to take my leave.

Star Trek Farewell

Fitting finale to a famous race,
James Noonan's ashes blasted into space.

Flight 93

i.m. Todd Beamer

Thousands the toll,
write on a scroll
two words, "Let's roll."

The Honeymooner

Philippe Petit walking a drum-taut wire
        above Niagara Falls,
        the lower canyon walls
encompassing the spray and man's desire

to wake, start off his days hell bent to strive,
        putting his past behind
        while centering the mind,
then go to bed more certainly alive.

Today I sit, a blank computer screen,
        still terrified of heights
        that frighten me some nights
but heightened by the waterfalls I've seen.

One thousand four hundred and forty feet,
        a quarter mile in air:
        acrophobes in despair
gazed up. That feat Petit would not repeat.

After the Twin Towers, what a lark!
he entertained children in Central Park.

Phlebas the Phoenician

Nobody witnessing my midlife spiral
far gone in alcohol thought I would live,
and though none of my verses have gone viral
now in my seventh decade I forgive

time before, after, the waste, sad time,
as said one I so studied in my teens
who really never gained my gift for rhyme
but looked deeply. Into those youthful scenes

it's hard to peer. I can't be seventeen.
Five decades on Eliot is a ghost,
a mist arising from a shipwreck scene
I captain. He's a reef, an iron coast,

and I lie windward with a broken rudder.
Veer out the oars. Too soon my keel will shudder.

Senior Patrol Leader

More wood crafty than any other boy
swiftly I rose through ranks,
four times yearly giving my thanks
for Wilderness, our pride and joy.
Boy Scouting is a pure democracy
and meritocracy.
Running my little troop
I gave no thought to popularity,
but saw my charges' spirits didn't droop
in snow or rain,
patiently teaching all we had to gain
from the North Woods,
distinguishing our shouldn'ts from our shoulds,
reading the field maps that an Eagle draws—
A Scout Is, more a prayer than just twelve laws.

Dream: Worship at Wilderness

Building a tipi and a council fire,
we douse the kindling with some kerosene.
Scouts, let our smoke signal devout desire
to climb to Heaven. Let the full moon sheen
on Bad Axe Lake mirror the prayers we mean.
Hovering, three archangels bless our blaze
and prophesy the coming End of Days.

Of twenty-four campsites, I camped in seven,
mature the birches, second growth the pines.
A prairie child coming here aged eleven
deepens devotion as his soul inclines,
his body scrambles at the foot of Heaven.
Your clothes are sodden and your tents are damp.
Welcome, Tenderfeet, to Wilderness Camp.

Lunar Dream

The luna is the queen to every moth,
its golden globes glowing from dusty wings.
To press them use your finest silver cloth.
I've pinned one to my windowsill. It sings

high praises to the twelve full moons, their names
Native American, each month a tune
sings me to sleep far past my worldly claims,
Harvest, Hunter, Strawberry Moon in June.

Yesterday marked our peak monarch migration.
Halted by stiff south winds an orange cloud
lee of a shelterbelt was holding station,
but let a luna weave my silken shroud,

saliva secreting a chrysalis
from which let me launch forth to lasting bliss.

Double Sonnet, Jerusalem

A Covenant

Jerusalem is just as much my home
as Rome.
Our Father promised Israel to the Jews,
old news
over three thousand years ago and counting,
mounting
proof ever since Nineteen Forty-seven
that Heaven
keeps promises that the Almighty makes
and takes
our Father's solemn word to Abraham
seriously. His Son became a lamb
to save the miserable wretch I am.

Next Year, Jerusalem

Come let us bow, bend low
before the God who made us.
A tree that knows no snow
nor sheds its leaves will shade us.
It thrives beside a stream
seen in King David's dream.

If today you hear His voice,
harden not your heart.
This day let us rejoice
and pray when we depart
His sacramental feast.
We in the West pray east,

wherever we may roam
Jerusalem our home.

Dream of the Father

I am that which I am,
and fallen Israel?
My Son has borne that lamb
home from the Gates of Hell.

You do not pray to me
but Mary and my Son
crucified on a tree.
With them you're nearly one,

and laws? Three of the Ten
you often disobeyed.
You rarely stray again,
I think you grow afraid

with every passing year.
I am content with fear.

The Cross

I've written "leafless tree"
too many times before,
but now mortality
steers toward a leeward shore

whose gravels I shall groove
lolling, no luffing wind
to save me when I've sinned.
I've still so much to prove

to justify a gift
proffered when I was young
and first tried to give tongue
to the tectonic shift

tearing at my green art,
so hesitant its start.

Memorial Day, 2017

for Richard Wilbur

I.

Some sixty years ago my red head grew
over towered by giants of World War II.
Today I've read Pericles's great oration
to Athens, his embattled city-nation,
first year of the Peloponnesian War
which would grind on more than two decades more,
then Lincoln's lament for the Union Dead.
Timmy can still recite what Lincoln said.

II.

A sage argues these are the greatest speeches
in all our oratory, for each teaches
amor pro patria, and each succeeds
in calling us to two deep human needs,
to hold hard to our history, to pray.
I have some flowers to lay on graves today.

III.

Last year I had just three soldiers to call
        and this year only one.
        Normandy to Verdun
they smashed through Adolph Hitler's armored wall.
Tomorrow morning is Memorial Monday,
and I shall pray *Sic transit gloria mundi*.

Their Finest Hour

Boxing Day, and the monster tidal wave
swept west to Ceylon, to Thailand north,
three hundred thousand sucked into the grave.
Two of our bold carrier groups set forth
to carry food, medicine, and relief
for Aceh's unimaginable grief.

Doctors and nurses, hundreds in their strong
naval determination put to sea.
Sea Stallion choppers did not need our long
runways to give swift wings to charity,
from every young marine a helpful greeting.
Europe convened a five star hotel meeting.

Semper Fi, less motto than a code
richly deserving of a martial ode.

—26 December 2004

Virtues of Repetition

Stevie and Sharon prayed
hard for their failing friend,
the two of them dismayed
I came so near my end,

prayed with their pastor too,
Bruce whom I never met.
I didn't have a clue,
beast in a caveman's net,

snarling and poked by spears,
meat hissing on hot rocks.
Slowly my mind now clears,
inured to daily shocks,

focused on winding stairs
and oft repeated prayers.

Lenten Suite

Joel: 2:3

"Rend not your garments but your hearts!"—
lesson a prophet imparts
every Ash Wednesday reading,
so passionately pleading
we repent our sorry ways
all the rest of our days.

Foes, swords in your sashes,
our shields are smeared with ashes.

Ash Thursday

Tomorrow I eat no meat,
just clam and salmon soup.
Come to my humble stoop,
I'll ask You *sit and eat*

just as George Herbert did
four hundred years ago.
I'll sweep my steps of snow,
of sins that You forbid.

Sixty-Seventh Lent

Ash Wednesday past, the first Friday in Lent:
  time to repent
serious sins from decades long since past
  and time to cast
eyes forward to Matthew, Mark, Luke, and John,
  time to move on.

It's time for penance, prayer, and generous alms,
  time to weave palms
as each day we read from the Book of Psalms.
  King David calms
the sinful soul and turns it to Holy Week.
  It's time to seek

the Holy Spirit each dawn for forty days,
season for guilt, season as well for praise.

EWTN Daily Mass

The *capellmeister* writes eight part motets
  and glorious quartets.
Today he's penned us a new Kyrie
starring the best cantor I've ever heard
  who sings the Holy Word
as world-wide viewers press their palms to pray.
  So do I start each day.

First Saturday

Moses: *The Lord your God*
publishes these decrees.
We rise from creaking knees,
my congregation, awed

to hear God as we must,
and Jesus's healing rain
falls on us in our pain,
the just and the unjust.

Luke 15:11–32

The prodigal son returns.
Slaughter the fatted calf
and strew the floors, with ferns.
Dance, make merry and laugh.

I too have made that turn
with some years yet to run,
a Lord for Whom I burn.
I know that prodigal son.

A gift: to reconcile
with sinners who repent
and make the angels smile,
that is the grace of Lent.

Matthew 4:1–11

Vade retro, Satanas,
Apage, Satanas,
your choice, Latin or Greek.
Picture a desert peak
with Satan and our Lord,
the abhorred and the adored.

No worldly wealth can tempt Him,
no argument preempt Him.
Fasting for forty days,
He foresees as in a haze
the hill of Calvary,
His corpse nailed to a tree.

April 9, 2017

Sunday our Hebrew forebears spread their palms
under the hooves of Jesus's milk-white ass
at the great gate in Jerusalem's walls.
Whoo-hoo in its descent a white dove calls
to Pharisees and beggars as they pass.
Christians, have you fasted and offered alms?

Five days hence Christ will be crucified,
then resurrected at the Easter Vigil
I have observed now for some dozen years.
The grim Centurions will rack their spears,
after my dark decades the vestigial
faith I once fled no more to be denied.

Lenten Instruction

Give alms, fast every Friday, read and pray.
You've seven sacraments to be your guide,
four gospels to pore over every day,
a daunting summons as our Savior's bride.

Make a truthful confession every night,
the moral inventory of AA,
then in your sleep may all your dreams take flight
to be remembered on your mundane way.

Your doctor hopes you have some decades left
to shape your soul before the Grand Assize.
Strive to invest your writings with a heft
worthy the craft. Give no thought to the prize

of wide acclaim. The ethic of hard work
learned in childhood, renew and never shirk.

Nightmare

I dreamed Satan had put our Lord in hock,
and I scrambled to scrounge among my rich
friends for the funds to break the pawn shop's lock
but couldn't raise them. This was an evil bitch,

and none of my prodigious skills in sales
opened a billfold, all of them glued shut,
a doomed sale where every strategy fails,
the pawn shop a dilapidated hut,

North University, its mansard roof
shedding its shingles and its windows soaped.
Vivid remembered details are my proof
that everything for which I prayed and hoped

came to nothing but Edvard Munch's *The Scream*,
for Satan was the author of my dream.

Xenophobia

Wildly was I red-haired
and freckled my pale skin,
and many bullies dared
daunt me, so small and thin,
swimming a Lutheran sea,
my goal eternity.

I grew in humbler times,
seed from an ancient bin.
Now men launch many crimes
at those with olive skin,
black, yellow, or brown,
common in my small town,

the fear of who is strange
the only thing we change.

Practice Often

Making the Sign of the Cross
so many times each day,
I clear my mind to pray.
I offer every loss,

struggle or minor gain
to Him who was hanged for me,
nailed to a leafless tree,
unthinkable His pain.

I used to meditate,
but my unquiet soul
rebelled, the heavy toll
of sin kept Heaven's Gate

veiled in a cloud of grey,
not so now when I pray.

A Line of Advice

Gods often go in travelers' disguise.
        They are ravelers
        and unravelers
of legendary truths, even of lies,
and the gods can bestow an unseen blessing.
        Peasant attire,
        welcoming fire,
ellipses in their speech to keep you guessing—
consider, friend, Baucis and Philemon,
        Hermes and Zeus,
        the frantic goose,
the ruin Zeus rained down upon their town,
two trees in their entwining limbs caressed.
Hospitalis—the Murphy Family Crest.

Return to China, an Ode

The Meditator

The Mahayana meditate in dream
under Mount Kailash. From its glacial snow
seeking the ocean, called The Encircling Stream,
Indus, Karnali, Brahmaputra flow.

Milarepa, god poet of Tibet
contemplates his crystalline cave alone.
Four mighty lamas venerate him yet,
seated on fabled pinnacles of stone.

I've used many mantras to meditate.
Now I silence the Sanskrit in my mind
better to bolster my exalted state
and see clearly the secrets I would find.

Breathing slowly, I try to visualize
the look of love in Milarepa's eyes.

The Belt of Heaven

First drill and screw three triple L-shaped hooks
right through the saw horse and your plywood paddle.
One hundred fifty strands of kite string silk
yield you a half-inch cincture white as milk,
or stain it ocher with a dyer's raddle.
You have not seen this done in any books.

Wind, tamp, and the rope will shrink two thirds,
back splice for show, whipping will just not do.
I wear mine with a grand Tibetan robe
a phoenix brought me halfway round the globe,
brocade embroidered in a golden hue,
daggers, dragons too delicate for words,

the swastikas, symbols for Mount Meru.
I wear it when I'm reading to the birds.

Chinese Studies

I had one insight in my teenage years,
China would put its Century of Tears
behind it and rival us in the East,
that Asia would become a Szechuan feast.

I read Confucius, Lao-tze, and Chuang-tzu,
no green tea, an intoxicating brew,
my *I Ching* studies teaching me that change
is constant, Mencius-rich, and strange,

history starting in the Shang and Han
centuries when the Greeks woke to their dawn.
Then three great poets, all T'ang Dynasty,
Li Po, Du Fu, finally Po Chu-i,

I cast their poems to the Encircling Stream,
moon bridge, rice paper, and a boyhood dream.

Friendship

I come in praise of China's New Silk Road,
 of Chairman Xi Jinping
 and deathless T'eng Xiao Peng,
leaders who lifted China from its load,
the cruel, crushing hand of Chairman Mao
who had scant understanding of the Tao

that treasures change but honors its restraints.
 China, go lay new rails,
 ship after ship that sails
waterways to the West. Confucius paints
like Lao-tzu and Chuang-tzu a shining path
for those who would transcend the sin of Wrath.

Over Pangea's deep tectonic rift
I send friendship, a lowly poet's gift.

Strength to Change

"Sicknesses of despair":
addiction, suicide,
I nearly perished there.
It was a rocky ride.

Lord, let me fill my time
with relished memories
in meter and in rhyme
of boyhood in the trees,

of manhood on the Plains,
and nearby Beartooth range
which seeds our needed rains.
Grant me the strength to change.

Kailash Manasarovar Yatra

South face of Kailash there's a crystal cave
        at nineteen thousand feet
        and on his sacred seat
Milarepa, a Buddhist world to save.

Mount Gurla Mandhata lies not far.
        When I am most bereft
        Rakshastal on my left
and to my right Lake Manasarovar

compose my meditation, Yellow Hat.
Thinking of happiness, I think of that.

To the General Secretary

Xi Jinping, let Liu Xiaobo,
dying of cancer, go.

Shambala

Shambala which we translate Shangri-la,
        the Western Paradise,
        lies where the mountains rise
to heights we can't conceive of. Ravens caw

aloft yellow canola on a plain
        blooming beneath its peaks
        where I am one who seeks
my answers to the whys of human pain.

There glaciers feed the waterfalls and streams,
        headwaters that will pour
        wherever hearts grow sore
in those who find their refuges in dreams.

The Seekers

for Alex Kerr

Was it Chuang Tzu dreaming of a butterfly
or a butterfly dreaming of Chuang Tzu?

Six noble bodhisattvas walked the earth
twenty-five hundred years before my birth,
no parallel in human history,
coevals? It's a cosmic mystery.
God Consciousness, what such a one achieves,
happens so rarely that its bearer leaves
on the wide fields of men a lasting path
to steer us from our bloody-minded wrath.

The Buddha sat under the Bodhi tree
calves crossed, a foot propped upon either knee,
meditating forty-nine days and woke
Enlightened, unburdened of his human yoke.
I thought myself Buddhist for twenty years,
two long decades in which I shed no tears,
a refuge when I had no place to go.
He still lights in my heart a loving glow.

Meanwhile Confucius wrote his *Analects*
little concerned with warring tribes or sects,
a system founded on the family,
a state grounded in filial piety.
From him I learned my reverence for the old
whose warmth drew me, a creature from the cold,
my long perspective on tumultuous Change
I've never found frightful nor even strange.

Some think me Master of the Shang *I Ching*.
Near fifty years I've heard three quarters ring,
falling upon a desk or table top,
myriad texts revealed by how they drop.
Fortune telling? Not so, it is a tool
to purge folly from a self-seeking fool.
To search the commentaries of its seers
Confucius longed to live a thousand years.

The *Tao Te Ching*, Great Book of the Way
ascribed by China to the sage Lao Tse,
founder of Taoism, another fruit
of Chinese wisdom, it had taken root
in my dark heart, heart of my lover too
when we lay blinkered, little hope in view
during the decades we were groping east,
shunning our natal sacramental feast.

Pythagoras taught us geometry
so equilateral in its symmetry.
Plato's great forebear moved to Italy
to live a life of extreme poverty.
Sandals he donned were never made of hide
but hemp, and he was never known to ride
donkey or horse. Once measuring a tree
this Boy Scout made his theorem a part of me.

We Christians search the elder Testament
for signs of Christ's coming, but I resent
how far some stretch to twist an ancient text
to serve their expectations, and my next
task is to find the truth, and it is there.
For two prophets, rising from their despair
over their sorry selves and Israel,
lived in their lives the Harrowing of Hell.

The Babylonian Captivity
was black time for the Jews, but prophecy
reached its apex under our seer Isaiah,
his young contemporary, Jeremiah,
whose text from David, "Like unto a tree
beside a stream," was Alan's obsequy.
I thank the Lord six sages walked the earth
twenty-five hundred years before my birth.

IV.
Late Spring

Letter to Belmont

i.m. Richard Wilbur

Master, I reread Monsour's "Burrowing Bees"
and learned today you're in a nursing home
far from the Berkshire woods you used to roam.
I hope you have a view of turning trees.

Mr. Warren directed me to you,
"The best we've got," thirty-nine years ago,
half of a lifetime as the red leaves blow.
Your letters told just what I had to do:

"Charge your language," "accurate observation,"
"precise expression" equal to each task.
I hunt today, sipping my whiskey flask.
None of your juniors have achieved your station,

Mr. Parnassus being the name I gave
Mount Wilbur, scrambling up your lower slopes,
wild with ambition and frustrated hopes,
mastery seeming distant as the grave.

For now your large family is close by,
so many visitors, much merriment.
Long may the silkworm weave your cerement,
blue as the sea, Lord, make the Belmont sky.

Today I quarter our Sheyenne River banks,
number my debts, and now I pray for you,
after four decades more I cannot do
but write in my red head this note of thanks.

Postscript
Richard, the word just reached me very late
you have passed on to claim your rich reward
for ten decades of service to our Lord.
I trust Charlotte was waiting at the Gate.

—15 October 2017

Postcard from Cummington

Dick's highest praise for poems was "well turned,"
    nod to the potter's wheel,
    and much like forging steel
dripping clay from the wheel is slowly burned

in the hot fire of a kiln to gain its glaze,
    to fix its pigment fast,
    an artifact to last
long past its patient maker's numbered days.

For me the metaphor is hunting, "bagged,"
    a pheasant in the grass
    flushed where my gun dogs pass,
or a fly ball my young outfielder shagged.

The point is, poet, what you must do, do well.
The making of middling verse is middling hell.

Three Songs for David

Lord of Belmont

In David Berman's forested backyard
the show I'm watching goes all morning long.
High in his trees each robin trills its song,
but Thomas Turkey is wooing pretty hard.

Two hens trailing no little schools of poults
try to ignore him, turning their brown backs.
In our lifetimes this wood has feared no axe,
its only hazard random thunderbolts.

On full display sized like a dining chair,
beard impressive, young Tom has little wattle.
Stately the only setting for his throttle,
he struts his stuff as if I weren't there,

a gallinaceous prince of just last year
and Lord of Belmont where he knows no fear.

Timothy Murphy

i.m. David Berman
1935–2017

David, friend and my superlative host,
you have been kidnapped by the Holy Ghost.
Let me comfort Margaret in her loss,
and may your long devotion to Christ's cross
whisk you straight up to Heaven. Your long toil
in the vineyard, hoeing our weedy soil,
should breeze you past St. Peter at the gate.
Alas, you've left too early, not too late.

I dream your boat departs the Plymouth shore
in a calm sea, no crashing breakers roar,
your mourners dabbing tears despite their smiles,
your destination is the Fortunate Isles
where three tall queens wearing their silver helms
walk with King Arthur under the leafing elms.

Timothy Murphy

Which of the Arts You Mastered

Which of the arts you mastered—through a life
rich in accomplishments—defines you best?
The lawyer's art, that talent you possessed
for finding order where disorder's rife,
in human judgment? Or your scholar's way
with words—those of Lucretius or Saint Paul,
or ours—you studied? You enriched them all.
Or your musician's gift for making play
out of the labor of confronting pain?
Wit, poet, verbal jeweler, and much more:
oenologist and gourmet chef whose door
opened with joy, who said, "Come soon agayne,"
like that, to friends who mourn you. As we should.
Come soon agayne indeed. We wish you could.

Rhina P. Espaillat

January 25, 2017, an Ode

My Students

Two hundred kids bussed to the March for Life.
        Worried husband and wife
wonder are they securely chaperoned?
        Their mental muscles toned
by Scripture, Confirmation, the Sacraments
        and King David's laments
learned at each Friday Mass, oh cut them loose,
Irish and Scots children. Robert the Bruce,
        come storm forth from your grave,
so little time, so many teens to save.

Minus 25 F

It's Burns Day, thc Conversion of St. Paul,
so it's doubly a holy day for me.
Lord, gird my loins in sheer temerity
as with redoubled reverence I call
poet and saint from heaven's unseen wall
where both long since passed to infinity,
unity with the Holy Trinity,
while earthbound on my frozen fields I crawl.

Westlin Winds

Westlin Winds,
count not my sins
upon the bloomin' heather.
The hawk and owl,
they fluff and scowl
in this inclement weather.

Though born to beg,
I've no sweet Peg,
no lass to lie beside me.
Though rocks may run,
melt wi' the sun,
I've whiskey to betide me.

Oh wake me to
a montane view
far from this endless prairie.
The boy I knew
and bade adieu
grew old and couldn't tarry.

Back in Class

Irish poems: it is St. Patrick's Day,
first The Breastplate and then Eileen Aroon
which I must somewhat tremulously croon,
then the young Yeats, "When You Are Old and Grey,"
"Wandering Aengus," then poems of his old age
I speak by heart with no help from a page.

Too young to comprehend The Second Coming,
the horrors of our bygone century,
a hundred million dead, a battery
of guns booming until our ears were drumming,
but Sailing to Byzantium we'll pick,
an agèd man not propped upon a stick.

I'll wrap up with my favorite youthful Heaney
and for my younger hunters, best of Feeney.

My Vikings

for Steve Syrdal

Their rune for O bears three strings like a harp,
the only rune I can easily read.
Their swords, corroded, once were ever sharp
and ran red with the blood their foes would bleed.
Their helms were inlaid, horned or winged like gulls,
and dragon prows glared proudly from their hulls.

I am one-fourth Norwegian. My red hair
comes out of Ireland, raped by the wild Norse
who never met a foe they didn't dare
engage and vanquish with berserker force,
however many perished in the deep,
the whale roads or the barrows where they sleep.

Thoroughbreds

I think *shirks* is the perfect rhyme for *works*,
dead opposites, I've used it once before.
When duty calls, the drone work-shirker lurks
in shade, evades the ardor of his chore.

This summer half our teens are unemployed,
predicament unheard of in my day.
I pity boys who never have enjoyed
aching muscles after a mowing day.

The nation needs jobs at an entry wage,
harder the better. Let the boys fell trees,
girls babysit, their supervisors gauge
these sovereign antidotes to miseries

for youths glued to a screen when they are idle,
who don't break from a gate with bit and bridle.

MDG

Always thirteen days' senior in this art,
fostering me since first I made my start
across our western stage, driving my cart

up the Missouri to the Great Divide
high above tree line where the marmots hide
and Christ is lamplit by his loyal bride,

both of us sons of the unlettered West
starting as teens on an unlikely quest
to be weighed in the balance as a test,

your hair grows silver, mine is still aflame,
but each of us set forth to nail a name
on a cathedral door, to stake a claim.

Pitching camp for the coming of a Guest
we waste little daylight before we rest.

David, Meet Mr. Lincoln

for Paul Lake

The days of man are grass?
On the High Plains the grass runs on forever
until the ice returns. It is man's endeavor,
his dreams that swiftly pass.

Wait, wait for the Lord.
Well, wait at least *four score and seven years,*
a span of life for me that slowly nears.
Then I shall be restored,

this I believe, I know.
Leaving the trailhead of my final track,
I shall give thanks that I have turned my back
on blowing, drifting snow.

Reader, indulge my books after I go.

4 July 2017

So I begin my sixty-seventh Fourth,
the needle on my leaf still pointing north
but oriented east by four degrees,
and I begin my day on grateful knees,
my first reading Jefferson's Declaration.
Thank God that I was born into this nation.

Then I read Charlie Cooke in NRO
who swam thc Pond against the Gulf Stream's flow
and reads more deeply than my countrymen
Framers whose like we shall not see again
but whose aspiration stays with us still,
John Winthrop's "shining city upon a hill."

Rewind

Cathy, you're still so ill.
I wish there were a prayer,
wish that I had a pill
and a half-storey stair

to lead you back to youth,
the pink flush on your cheek,
but dear, to tell the truth
it is our graves we seek,

those and the granted grace
startling us every day,
staring us in the face.
Your hair has long grown grey,

your brow and throat are lined.
We've no time to rewind.

Freshman Physical

In the Payne Whitney Gym
a naked shivering boy:
a coach I would destroy,
instantly hated him.

Told that I have kyphosis,
told I must stand up straight,
the advice came too late.
Still suffer from lordosis.

Had to do thirty pushups,
ten pull-ups on the bar,
tests I could clear by far
with my one hundred sit ups.

Last test the pool, long swim,
I was exempt from gym.

Stream of Unconsciousness

Wake by a river
reach for a quiver
shadows you shiver

reach for an arrow
ghouls from a barrow
aim small and narrow

swear forever
that you will dissever
desire from endeavor

to put things level
flush on the bevel
and cast the devil

out in the cold
exhausted and old.

This Works Every Time

Climbing, no stream in spate
to get you through your drouth,
roll pebbles in your mouth,
and you will salivate.

Let them be rounded, three
sufficed me when the worst
came of a mountain thirst
in my extremity.

Above, the torrent's roar,
below, the aspen trees,
here but the gasping breeze
where wheeling vultures soar—

so did Demosthenes
become an orator.

Standing Bear

We name him Standing Bear.
The distance in his stare
encompasses the West.
Centuries are no test
for one who rears on guard.
I am his minor bard.

I've seen him in Alaska
and glimpsed him at Itasca.
I've seen him in Wyoming,
Montana, in my roaming
his realms, the tree-line heights
that haunt my prairie nights,

a star-crossed peak where he
chases me up a tree.

Study in Black

Shootout on Main Street where he always wins,
postponing punishment for all his sins,
sidearm, ivory-handled forty-five,
none of his former foemen left alive,

the villain of a thousand Western scenes,
his weathered leather chaps low on his jeans,
his boots unpolished with their tarnished spurs,
unbeliever for whom no angel whirrs,

cloud over his head, his visage grim,
he rides through Deadwood where the light is dim.
In cowboy hat and a black dustcoat clad
he's lost his shadow, the last thing that he had.

The *Scop*

ond sawol secgan
sothfastre dom

Have you a *wyrd*,
have you a *dom*,
have you a sword?
I am a *scop*,
ever I roam.
Verses I grope
crushed to a page
stained with my blood,
the more that I age
run like a flood.
Maker of rhyme,
talker of tales,
born out of time,
hunter of whales.

The Wound

She had to carve out three inches of skin
down to the bone and muscle of my shin.
New skin took three months for its growing in.

This started out as just a dead stick scratch,
three one inch Band-Aids, they were my only patch,
but the biota came from a fecal batch,

and two weeks later it was a purple wound.
Looking at it the surgeon nearly swooned.

Three months later, bandaged from toe to calf,
it healed and I could look at it and laugh,
just another November hunting gaffe.

I said from memory Hardy's "The Wound."
"I'll never write that well," I sadly crooned.

i.m. Sam Shepherd

One movie pays for five plays.

I grieved deeply today, learning he died,
man of my generation. I took pride
in every shoot-out he bestrode in stride.

My favorite film of his is "Purgatory."
In "The Right Stuff," Sam Shepherd took the glory
for breaking the sound barrier, stole the story

in "Streets of Laredo," probably Shepherd's best
role, where an old James Garner lays to rest
villains, a brilliant actor's toughest test,

my old pen pal McMurtry's masterpiece.
I watch it when it's time to work bear grease
into my boots while playing without cease

a score by Poledouris, "Lonesome Dove,"
the greater sister movie that I love.

Happy Birthday, J.R.R.

Today *The Hobbit* turns eighty years old.
          We read *Lord of the Rings*
          in high school, Shelob's stings
making us flinch. Beside his fireplace, cold,

Auden opened his Anglo-Saxon teacher
to greet Bilbo, a most courageous creature,

for six hours straight standing, immersed in thought.
          England was Middle Earth,
          Black Stone my country's birth.
Heroes and villains, so religion taught.

Reader, like Auden turn page after page,
books can be judged great at a distant age,

then delve deeply *The Silmarillion*
and dream backward to Homer's Ilion.

Je connais

My favorite cognac is the Hennessy,
et bien sûr, make it dear V.S.O.P.,
tied for second Courvoisier and Martel,
elixirs which can claw me up from Hell.
        Burgundy or Bordeaux?
          An aged merlot
or pinot noir, my merchant knows my vines,
I tasted fifty to select two wines,
but all of these simply amateur hour,
Dickel the soul of any whiskey sour.
I lie, all of my liquor I drink neat
with a fresh poem panting at my feet.

How Shall I Drink All This?

Tanha, craving, I know which is my worst,
whiskey by which the words within me burst
in metered torrents, lines ending in rhymes
recounting both my worst and best of times.
No alcoholic ever lived so long
borne on the wings of whiskey and of song.

Fargo to Ulaanbaatar

Two cashmere coats,
maybe six sweaters,
I have no betters.
Tell me, dear goats,
on your treeless plain
have you some rain

to make your grass lush,
better to graze
on lengthening days?
Do the gales shush?
Doves on the wing,
here comes our spring,

I send my smiles
six thousand miles.

First Nightmare

A little boy, I wafted out of bed
to the crown corner molding of my room
until my nose was pressed to it. The gloom
all lightless would frighten my little head,
claustrophobic the confines of my dream.
My parents came the second I would scream.

Roughly four years this nightmare I endured.
Now I can find no reason for those frights
inflicted on me all too many nights,
that cornering, I never grew inured,
but soul and body's unity restored
I'd sleep again. Last night I softly snored,

that nightmare now banished for sixty years,
my pillow rarely dampened by my tears.

Thysells, an Ode

Strophe, Dancing with Death

Pitch pole: Jim did it on a Hobie Cat,
Brian and he totaled two hundred pounds,
a force five gale that didn't knock them flat
but buried bows to teach two boys their bounds.

They probably exceeded thirty knots,
thirty-three miles an hour, way too fast,
a speed undreamed of by my stately yachts.
They were lucky that sail was not their last.

Both little guys were flung into the shrouds,
badly abraded when the Hobie flipped,
mast head in lake-bed. Over them the clouds
rolled in the gale. Ashore their spotter shipped

binoculars and roared forth in his launch.
They learned three meanings of a new word, staunch.

Antistrophe I, Viva II

A nor'east breeze, and John Thysell turned green,
retired below to hug the head for hours.
The fetch to Canada, a placid scene,
but swells ran huge, and rolling to their powers

dead downwind, hard to hold the rudder true,
danger of jibing and our progress slow
as round and round wound our small diesel's screw,
disengaged, neutral all it would know

that long day south athwart Madeleine Isle.
Those swells above our boom return in dream,
and I grew much as helmsman that long while
we rolled southwest on Lake Superior's stream

I think it was forty-six years ago.
When young we can't foresee how we shall grow.

Antistrophe II, Nana

Lucky Thysells, they had a live-in granma
expert at baking cookies, painting rocks.
Her story I don't know, all called her Nana,
and she was sovereign for our childhood shocks.

John's older brother Steve was a young god,
so tall, so handsome, well, I was just little.
I never golfed with him, too overawed,
my slice so wicked and my backswing brittle.

Ten of us in eight years, tribe beside tribe,
Vance and Vincent our fathers, the two V's
to whom our manly virtues we ascribe
although our mothers dipped us in the seas

of Big Floyd Lake where summers we still gather,
sister and sister, moms, brother and brother.

Epode: Kinko's

Our John a secret genius, scary smart,
        but where such cunning comes
        with neither fifes nor drums
defeats the story telling of my art.

The U of M, east side the Mississippi,
        he built a copy shop
        where profs and students drop
pennies for copies, both preppy and hippy.

Built them in college towns across the Plains,
        Xerox the mighty weapon
        to make his fortune happen.
In high school he was not acclaimed for brains

but beauty and gymnastics, second son
cashed out by FedEx from his fabled run.

The Varian Disaster

A German princeling held hostage by Rome
grew great in the legions. Going home
he grieved, seeing how downcast were his *volk*,
living enslaved under the Roman yoke.

Germania, not an aqueduct or town:
I ask did Arminius crave a crown?
In Rome he could be no more than a knight,
genius at warlike tactics, reared to fight.

Immune to Roman baubles and their bribes,
he forged the Rhineland and its warring tribes
to slaughter in the forest and the marsh
three legions when the elements were harsh.

Centuries later, still enraged with wroth,
they marched on Rome, Vandal, and Visigoth.

—Teutoburg Forest, 9 A.D.

Joel's Willow

Old willow, last of our trees to shed your leaves
and even worse your twigs
each of which worms, then digs
into the snow, each fall my spirit grieves,

seeing your greenery go.
How on earth do you blow
your leaves clear to my yard?
A gale from the southeast
huffing and puffing like a ravening beast
strips bare your slender limbs it blows so hard.

Boreas never taught that wind to sing
but strum your lofty lyre
to which our squirrels aspire.
There will be time to rake your mess come spring.

Senior Year, 1968

Seidel should have been our Class President.
        He was six four and blond,
        waving his slender wand
to win every basketball tournament.

Every Class President had been a jock.
        I won instead, a nerd
        gifted in every word,
second rebuttals, times to gently mock.

Three girls, three proms hosted by different schools,
        I knew what *mauvaise foi*
        meant, what it took to claw
Tim into Yale and drub its preppy fools,

my highest joy, the fire by which I burned
and the lines I so tortuously turned.

Three Thanksgivings

Agapē in Moorhead

At Day House it's a grand Thanksgiving dinner,
like you every attendee is a sinner,
a battered woman or a homeless drunk,
bring light to each eye so sadly sunk.
Come Catholic, carve and serve the basted bird
and do so with a smile, a Christian word
of kindness. To Blessed Dorothy Day
so soon to be sainted let us pray.

Military Honors

Bloodied hands bearing a body bag,
then six white gloves fold a tricorner flag,
ten white gloves will fire three carbine rounds
over a graveyard where no zephyr sounds
its whispers on a funereal day
under our wide sky be it blue or grey,
the colors that our warring armies wore
to tear our nation in the Civil War.
This ceremony can surpass the Mass
preceding it, for so our valiant pass.

Another Thanksgiving Prayer

Dear Lord,
I pray too seldom for our troops,
fresh-faced Middies racing their low blue sloops,
their seniors sailing off beneath the sea,
nuclear-armed, swiftly and silently,
eleven crews, each of six thousand men
and women, all being deployed again
on carriers, the pilots of their planes,
Special Forces making our hard-earned gains,
ten thousand soldiers in Afghanistan
sixteen long years after that war began
and fifteen in Iraq, our engineers
grinding their armored dozers through their gears,
Marine Guards posted from Beijing to Rome,
safe in Your hand hold them and bring them home,

Amen

Timothy

My name eponymous with just one thing,
Timothy, high hay with a lovely ring,
name of a flawless poem by Tim Steele
lodged in my memory, it makes me feel
the ache of muscles swinging their curved scythe,
transported five decades I'm lean and lithe.

Lover of mowing poems, Robert Burns,
Frost, Marvell, and Alec Hope who turns
his scythe to meditate on Father Time,
sinuous lines each with its perfect rhyme,
dactyls and anapests, hear how they lope.
Aged forty-five I coped with Alec Hope.

Boyhood, manhood, sweating under the sun,
I've praised the grass much as I've praised my gun.

Very Far North in My Closet

This tan jacket trooped to England with me
to hear me read, Royal Festival Hall,
then Christ Church, the Auden Society,
then Grasmere where I answered Wordsworth's call
and said Intimations from memory.

Its blue blazer brother came with us too,
likewise cashmere, silk ties three inches wide.
Here are my corduroys, a paler blue,
in which this shrunken man could nowadays hide
glad that he still has no white head to rue.

Twenty-five years past my first voyage there,
and Murphy had a second book to read
published in London, reeking of despair,
like thirty pounds which I no longer need.

Sixty-something

I like what happens to my dreams, my mind,
          my eyes that grow less blind,
but loathe what is happening to my frame
          which slowly grows more lame,

severely cutting back my hunting time.
          It's easier to rhyme,
an art I've practiced nearly fifty years.
          I love the star that steers

my footsteps at the darkness of the moon
          where oftentimes I croon
to music not perceived when I'm awake
          and sailing on a lake,

beating to windward where I don't recall
my nightly scramble up high Heaven's wall.

That Dream Again

That dream again, a passage underground,
        perhaps a movie house
        where like a blinded mouse
I grope fearful of every scrabbling sound,

thence to a hall of floor to ceiling glass
        where blinking in the sun
        I have a mile to run
down many passageways which I must pass

while meting out a French epic in verse,
        and then I start my climb
        up scaffolding, grim time
for such an acrophobe, the final curse

to flex my fledgling wings, trying to fly,
but plummet like a stone thrown from the sky.

New Year's Eve 2017

Turn of the year, time for "The Darkling Thrush"
and young Greg Williamson's "The Mockingbird,"
reply to Hardy, poems not read but heard
from the mind's mother file in evening's hush,
masterpieces one hundred years apart,
two of the myriad poems I have by heart.

My father spoke "The Darkling Thrush" to me.
Greg's bird sang to a blaring car alarm
twelve hundred miles from my snow-covered farm,
meditations on time, mortality
overcome by a song, "some blessed hope
whereof he knew." Lord, lend me strength to cope

with darkness and a poem as good as these
to be graven in others' memories.

V.
Still Farming All Night

Elpis

Hope is the thing with feathers
that perches in the soul.
Brave child, she somehow weathers
the thunderstorms that roll

over the frightened prairie.
We look up at the sky,
our denizens all wary
of promises. We cry,

"Your symbol is an anchor
eye spliced to a rope,"
and some of us feel rancor
when we're betrayed by Hope.

September 4, 1988

By a Chinook wind warmed
a mesocyclone formed,
spooling down from the Plains;
for all that we endured
soybeans would be interred.
Gwinner got tardy rains,

but Drought of Eighty-eight?
The rain came far too late,
our row crops doomed to fail.
A dear friend long inured
to trials, much insured,
Kelly danced in the hail.

Montana Idyll, a Dream of the West Yellowstone

A ranch with hip-roofed barns and sprawling halls:
a pony whinnies on his slender tether,
some fifty feet of braided, weathered leather
on which he roams outside the stable stalls.
He leads a good life being this rancher's horse,
gentled to bridle, saddle, not by force.

Under the burden of an apple tree
whose lower fruit I snatch with a small jump,
lies spreading shade over an iron pump
and stock tank where two Labradors roam free.
This valley leaves the visitor agog.
Not a bad life being this rancher's dog.

Tow-headed kids and an adoring wife,
lucky the rancher who has found this life.

Giving Thanks

Our State Tree? It is the power line pylon.
Those monsters crossed my farm that we called Hammer,
bearing our coal-fired power to Minneapolis.
Hunting beneath them, high overhead a buzzing,
and on those wires, trust me, no bird alighted.
Said to be safe? Grateful I didn't live there.

North Dakota is so rich in resources,
coal, oil, and gas in the great Bakken Basin.
So God sustains six hundred thousand people,
but the chief, first font of our wealth is farming,
sixty-eight thousand sections where the glaciers
retreated, leaving us our level topsoil,

from the black loam of our Red River Valley
to the hard scrabble of our High Plains pastures.

Murphy Baked Beans

Great Northern, pinto, navy, and kidney beans,
    molasses and honey,
cook low. Counter-topped my crock pot leans
    north, and old friends make money

irrigating these choice, specialty crops
    southwest of our Valley.
In August's beans the combine never stops
    and glorious the tally.

I earned a hundred thousand dollar check
    from Walton Bean one year,
money to prop up my shambolic wreck.
    Twenty years I've steered clear.

Serve beans with a sautéed steak of ham,
or better yet, grill up a leg of lamb.

Sandwich Heaven

Nathan's Famous Hot Dogs just came to town.
        Grill them and they're beef red,
        halve them on sourdough bread
(English muffins) with Grey Poupon to drown

New Zealand butter slathered onto your roll,
        your cheddar Kerrygold
        imported, and I've told
all that you need to know to sweep your soul

to sandwich heaven where the angels sing,
        serving their Irish cheese
        and dogs piled as you please
for lunch, bearing their platters wing on wing.

Breadsmith on 32nd

Morning croissants are butter-berry-bombs,
        Smuckers Preserves in fact,
        strawberry (be exact),
served with strong coffee, how this pastry calms.

Fargo has yet to bake a great baguette.
        I farmed the finest wheat
        man was designed to eat,
but perfect boules? Shop and be in my debt.

Sourdough, the art at which my friend excels,
        old San Francisco strain,
        bread to rebuild the brain
bought at dawn to inhale the oven's smells,

and while you're there try Rob's cranberry muffins,
my Holy Grail, eldest of all MacGuffins.
Just microwave until the butter softens.

Navigable Waters of the U.S.

Let them think twice before they use their powers
To blot out and drink up and sweep away
These flowery waters and these watery flowers
From snow that melted only yesterday.

My favorite poem is Robert Frost's "Spring Pools,"
but plant no wheat, nor God forbid! picked rocks,
they're inland waterways the farmer mocks
at his dire peril. Though no minnow schools,

dry fifty weeks a year, tadpoles can hatch
and hop into the fields, then estivate
in autumn mud, come spring resuscitate,
and government stands guard on every batch.

I once piled picked rocks on an old stone pile.
Heavily fined, years later I can smile.

Deliverance in June

Last night our people got a goodly rain
        falling upon the just,
        settling the planting dust.
Our farmers' labors won't have been in vain.

The grass was turning brown, showing the strain,
        the crops in cracking crust
        at risk of going bust,
a growing season squandered for no gain.

The liquor of despair tempts those in haste.
        Before this, every storm
        threateningly would form
but roll east to the lakes, ungodly waste.
        Now every rooting corm
can take a sip of mercy's summer taste.

Three Nightmares in One

A small black dog is pawing at my door.
        Shut out in the cold,
        arthritic, growing old,
I am that dream dog, and my maple floor

heaves like the deck of a two-masted ship
        beating around the Horn.
        This is a dream forlorn
of hope, a nightmare out of which I'd slip

to wake unscathed, but dreams can wreak deep harm
        and leave one drenched in sweat.
        This is not over yet.
Soon it will run to ruin on the farm,

the Drought of Eighty-eight, an evil book
through which only in dream I'm forced to look.

Specialty Crops

Both high oleic and confectionary,
bug spatter on a windshield, it was scary,
        the load could be rejected,
        our young drivers dejected,
expensive sunflowers cruelly crushed for oil,
vastly slashing the risk reward for toil.

For tofu I grew my gigantic beans,
for sprouts my wee ones. From our harvest scenes
        all were bound for Japan,
        containers, and I can
recall the triumph of those giant checks
which warded from the farm so many wrecks.

My best specialty crop was navy beans.
Let's fix beans and bacon to stretch your jeans.

Still Farming All Night, an Ode

That Dog Don't Hunt

Pasta-grade durum is damn hard to raise;
most years my ample rains
so unlike the High Plains
stunted my protein, and the August blaze

of sunlight came too late, not so spring wheat
ready some two weeks faster.
Barring a hail disaster
our flour made whole wheat whole cities could eat.

Similarly, barley of malting grade
escaped me, only feed
grain that Canadians need
flowed from my fields, no beer Budweiser made.

Three decades since I sold my fertile fields
I'm still praying my friends have bumper yields.

Pheasants of 1989

I only took my banker hunting twice.
    Timothy didn't shoot him,
    didn't Redwing boot him,
good young borrower I was really nice.

I lent him my first Model 23.
    A big black Angus ass
    could quite securely pass
at thirty yards he shot so errantly.

A balance sheet of brick he brought to town.
    I was his first big client,
    desperately compliant
as he poured forth the funds for me to drown.

Still Farming All Night

The filthiest of all jobs on the farm?
    Borrowing from a bank.
    For twenty years I sank
in dream, waking up to the same alarm.

Interest, two grand each day, was bleeding me,
    worse than the floods or droughts.
    I had six million doubts.
Neither a borrower nor a lender be.

The Toughening

Farming truly toughens a young man up
just as a shock collar corrects a pup.
Go to an anvil and lay down your balls,
then when you dream you will be climbing walls.
"Equity ratio should equal age,"
said Kelly who enlivens many a page
of searing drought, ruinous thunderstorm,
pages that you can burn to keep you warm
when all else fails, you buy books by the box
and your spring harvest is the winter's rocks
forced from the frozen clay up to the loam
that my Monsanto soybeans called their home.

Wet and Wetter

"That new three hundred sixty-five day corn,"
said Jimmy of some standing crop one spring.
One of the wettest falls since I was born
snowed in the corn our combines couldn't bring.

"Wet is always a bigger threat than drought"
Tommy Hartness who sold me my first farm.
Wheat lodging in hail tracks, every doubt
the young farmer can feel, every alarm

haunted me for the few years I would last,
fourteen. Now I pursue far different yields,
Chucky quartering on a frenzied cast
through cattail sloughs that used to be my fields.

Dream: Temple of Solomon

Down from the Temple stepped a goodly crowd,
all of them sowers, reapers of the wheat,
their faces beaming, their hosannas loud.
That winter they had bread enough to eat.

Beneath the Temple milled a shiftless mass
who'd slept through Sabbath, honored not their land.
For them calamity had come to pass,
all irrigators of the fertile sand.

"Say, shameless shirkers," cried the honored ones.
"have you no gifts to offer to the Lord?
The true he honors and the hapless shuns.
We rose at dawn, must He not be adored?

You'll stay His wrath with nonexistent yields?
The windlassed oxen watered not your fields."

Indian Summer

Our row crops really need a deep, hard freeze
as do the pheasant hunters, our soybeans
yet to be combined, shelling beneath these trees
blaze orange as my hunting vest and jeans,
the corn not yet fit for our propane driers,
this harvest topping all my friends' desires.

Three nights ago our low touched thirty-seven,
back to the forties with no end in sight,
slow-motion autumn, not a gift from heaven,
no full moon on its dreary, drizzling night.
Come on weather, take us to twenty-two,
and let our nights resume their starlit blue.

Past crops cut short by a too-early freeze,
now I pray for the first frost on my knees.

Green, a Double Sonnet

I think I've planted fifteen thousand trees,
more than most poets through the centuries.
—T.M.

Tree Islands

Two piles of giant, sawn-down cottonwoods
        felled twenty years ago
        have caught the soils that blow
in winter. Cock pheasants with crimson hoods

I've seen parading from surrounding beans
        to climb with stately ease
        these nurseries for trees,
seeds blown with the soil by human means,

tillage Kelly would minimize with ease,
        sparing the prairie streams
        I often hunt in dreams,
leaving our clods too large for gales to seize,

a revolution known as the chisel plough
which three generations are using now.

Second Green Revolution

I have seen street lights switching on at noon
        in a mid-winter gale.
        I watched the topsoil sail
over the sun. I was not born too soon
to see our farming change, to lend my hand,
trying to halt erosion on the land.

I have left green borders by tiny drains
        trickling from rolling fields
        at small cost to my yields.
That is why God has given farmers brains,
given us custody and made us green
long before urban zealots raised a scene.

I pray for scientists who crossbreed wheat
and see the world has bread enough to eat.

Cattle Prices

Much is depending on next year's calf crop.
Make it generous, grant the dry High Plains
 our badly needed rains,
we'll see this fall's near-record prices drop.

Strangely, short ribs are in shortest supply.
Most of my beef cuts are filet mignon.
 Cold leftovers at dawn,
then feed Chucky and scan the low, grey sky.

A second day I think we'll see stray flakes,
and yesterday my walk was slick, black ice.
 Very nearly slipped twice,
steadied with arms flung wide for my hips' sakes,

seven decades of practice to deploy.
I've no padding, a fall could cause grave harm.
 Take the boy from the farm,
but you can't take the farm out of the boy.

Peggy

"Losing? In farming it's a way of life,
the lifts are heavy, and the bumps are hard,"
I was told by a friend's long-widowed wife,
one I had never dreamed let down her guard.

"Too hot, too droughty or too cold and wet,
the seedbeds patchy where the grain drill skips,
noose round the neck, I feel it tighten yet.
The Four Horsemen of the Apocalypse

rode me into the ground, yet I survive
to see my grandsons carry on and farm.
Planting and harvest I feel so alive,
praying to ward away the next alarm,

praying before I sleep, after I wake.
Mark the snow geese wheeling above our lake."

Late Spring, an Ode

What Spring?

We've stinging snow on April Twenty-third,
not fit to trail a dog
into the swirling fog,
not fit for man, for beast, or warbling bird.

So dying winters deal us a *last, hard blow*,
and all dirt roads are mud
although they didn't flood,
nowhere my little Ford would care to go.

Just yesterday we saw two flowering crabs
by the Red River's banks,
a sight to summon thanks
from weather watchers keeping closest tabs.

Three days hence Chucky will take a stroll
to watch the tractors and the grain drills roll.

Wheat of 1984

Five days of cloud, never a glimpse of sun
or window to the blue,
and wintry is my view,
snow showering for Chucky's morning run.

Alan and I called Kelly April Fourth
that spring. Would Gwinner go,
forecast for heavy snow?
Kelly, inured to farming in the North,

planted a thousand acres in two days,
then nineteen inches dropped.
Of all the grains I've cropped
that was our best. Come golden August days

Kelly's fleet of Kenworths could not keep up
with five combines. I was one happy pup.

Late Spring

I'm starting to get worried for my old friends
who plant their beets and wheat
that hungry millions eat,
nothing but mud beside the rivers' bends.

May should be time for planting beans and corn,
but here no wheel has turned
however hearts have yearned
to get to the spring work for which we're born.

At least I don't have six million of debt
crushing my mortgaged soul,
but when the tractors roll
late, force of habit can oppress me yet.

Some crops are planted in the blow-dried sand,
but Fargo clay? I'm shackled to this land.

Crop Rotation, an Ode

Beans

Navies always fetched us a decent price,
        unlike the lowly soy
        whose markets brought no joy.
Two solid sections, I only grew them twice.

Kelly would solid seed, never in rows.
        No specialized machine,
        and after they turned green
they were no food for blackbirds, doves, and crows

feasting on our confectionary flowers
        which waited for a freeze,
        clear nights without a breeze,
prey to our migratory windblown powers.

First navy harvest thirty years ago.
Eat some bean soup, and feel your belly glow.

Wheat

Experiment: we planted winter wheat
        half January-killed.
        Come April Kelly drilled
spring seed which flourished in the showery heat.

That half breed crop gave me my highest yield
        in fifteen struggling years
        I was immune to tears,
twelve thousand bushels from one rocky field.

Twelve combines in an oak-framed photograph
        shot by my farmer's chopper,
        wheat topping every hopper,
decades later I look at it and laugh.

"Go home boy, sink your toes in that rich soil."
Badgering bankers is degrading toil.

Corn

I have a lifelong love affair with corn,
        the sweet corn in my youth
        delighting tongue and tooth,
my baby food soon after I was born.

I grew hundreds of acres in my day.
        My land could make it grow,
        but prices were so low
those losses cost me more than I can say.

I drive in summer just to watch it tassel
        high over my head
        and dream that when I'm dead
I'll climb the Rainbow Bridge to claim a castle

lonely as I, as windswept and forlorn,
and plough its pastures just to plant my corn.

VI.
Hiking All Night

Orchard in Bloom, woodcut by Charles Beck

North from Kenmare

With rapeseed left and flaxseed on my right,
    yellow and blue so deep
    they wake me from my sleep
and keep me half-enchanted half the night,

Saskatchewan: this is a youthful scene
    near Estevan, a road,
    backpacks our only load,
the Stetsoned drivers twenty-something lean,

come from first harvest of their bumper wheat
    as starboard raises dawn,
    north to *Alyeska* drawn
with ample jerkied venison to eat

and pumpjacks clanking in opposing fields
whose memories are my prodigious yields.

Directed Dreaming

I can direct a dream
home to Jerusalem
or to a montane stream,
twig to its river's stem.

I beg the Holy Spirit
before falling asleep
after my prayers, so near it,
the realm where dreams run deep.

I did this just last week,
two hunts in asphodel
with dead friends that I seek.
I greet Alan as well

and King David, his friend.
I glimpse my happy end.

A Gift

Proffered upon my knees,
a posture where I thrive:
a myriad of bees
have woven you a hive.

These bees work in the wild.
Foraging far from home,
from flowers undefiled
they made your honeycomb.

Listen: *Murmuring of*
innumerable bees.
That's Lord Tennyson, love,
no stranger to his knees.

General Aviation Day

Helicopter In

Alan wanted to see Assiniboine
        where Seppe and his wife
        pursued their alpine life,
their lodge scarcely in reach of my scant coin.

It's a dead ringer for the Matterhorn,
        four-sided pyramid,
        its upper reach forbid
to tyros. Giuseppe, to the manner born,

a Swiss Guide who migrated to the West
        led climbers to its peak,
        the Rockies all to seek.
Seppe thought it a goodly breakfast test.

I lurked below and fished the glacial pool
where brook trout leapt to fight my rod and spool.

Tim Navigates

Wahpeton, and Danny gassed up his bird,
easily half a mill,
then over dale and hill
we flew, headsets needed to speak a word.

We had to fly roughly two hundred miles.
Protractor on my map
(this was no time to nap)
and twenty knots of sideslip, with my wiles

we locked the yoke at west less ten degrees.
There on the chopper's nose
for all the wind that blows
lay the Jones farm, its bin site and its trees.

Not much different from piloting my yachts
except you sail more than a hundred knots.

Bush Pilot

He fled from Kalispell. It was too crowded.
His head and jaw were comfortingly clouded
in white. He sized up Alan's topo map:
"Never been tried." The chart in Alan's lap,
we flew northeast to test that virgin beach
under the Hubbard's face. I used to teach
map and compass, and said "Six hundred feet
right where the glacier and salt water meet,
this tail dragger can land there." Down we went.
With goal in mind Alan would not relent.
Three days later, take-off was pretty scary,
480 pounds of men and prairie
gear burdening that gutsy little craft
and bush pilot. Onward and never aft.

Unlicensed

Twenty degrees west of magnetic true
north I clutched my yoke. The little Cessna flew
down to its three-point landing. Skies were blue,

quartering headwind on the landing strip,
perfectly judged the small plane's sideways slip,
and yes, reader, I bit my lower lip.

This was no dream but thirty years gone by,
my first landing, pilot too drunk to fly,
reeking of bourbon, bloodshot his right eye,

take-off, left pedal counteracting torque,
Alan's computer landings for New York,
the whiskey flask I so longed to uncork,

my pilot slept nearly three hundred miles,
two more landings, each with broadening smiles
down over farmlands with their drainage tiles.

From Minot home lowering skies grew grey.
To quote my father, "I grew some that day."

Alan's House

South-facing window walls thirteen feet tall,
the roof, a redwood, brass-railed deck was flat,
bedazzled songbirds would fly splat and fall,
enticing Boots, our hungry young tomcat.

Out front were seven hundred apple trees,
out back the oxbow of the lazy Red.
Mow seated, graft the apples on your knees,
and wear a Stetson to protect your head.

I bought the land, and Alan planned two years,
drawing his mini-mansion masterpiece.
Over the crushing debt I dropped no tears,
but cancer came, our labors had to cease.

I sip Calvados, a VSOP,
and dream back to a blooming apple tree.

Two Thanksgivings

Two hours after our cold Thanksgiving dawn
twelve wild turkeys paraded on our lawn.
Raced to the gun rack, slammed two magnum two's
down Winnie's barrels, it was time to choose
store-bought bird or freshly slaughtered game.
No Butterball would ever taste the same.
But Alan wrenched the gun out of my hand,
"Tim! I'll allow no killing on our land
unless a rogue bunny has chomped a flower
blooming beneath our switchback staircase tower."

So Frost's great poem "There are Roughly Zones"
delimiting the bounds of mortal bones
and aspirations I muttered to myself
and boxed my ammo on its walnut shelf.
Twelve huge turkeys pecking near our pines,
today I'm giving thanks for sixteen lines.

—1 November 2017

Deference

On the White Mountains, later the Front Range,
Alan longed for everything high and strange.
His boats were homes, refinished and refurnished,
polish handy for all the brass he burnished.

Bone in his teeth, Alan's desire was fixed,
and any plan I had swiftly deep-sixed.
I was the Skipper, technically the boss,
seven years now how have I grieved his loss.

With King David he dwells among the saints,
I nightly pray to him with few complaints
and live on in a state of gratitude
for decades spent and this brief interlude

serving my time here among living men
till Alan calls all of our shots again.

78 Psalms

For a great work Alan was put on earth,
and nobody foresaw this at his birth,
to translate David into metered lines.
His final year in which the spirit pines
for unity with God he gave this work,
a daily duty he would never shirk
however strong the steroids in his veins,
however strong leukemia that drains
life from one's bones, however pained the nights
that no perfumed comforting candle lights.
No more long walks on Lauderdale's white strand,
ashes scattered at sea by my right hand.

Psalm Seventy-two

When David caused the death of Absalom
he settled firmly on King Solomon
and begged the Lord to make the youth His own,
to build His Temple and assume the throne
of Israel, to sire an endless line.
Alan's translation is especially fine:

> *Leave judgment with the king, O God;*
> *repose your virtue in his son*
> *that he may judge your people rightly*
> *and give fair measure to your poor.*

From David do we learn compassion.
Dear Lord, treat Alan in the fashion
accorded an evangelist.
Tell him how he is loved and missed.

Sierra Time

High up in the Sierra we got stuck,
snow to the windows of our Subaru.
I wedged branches under our tires, and luck
saw us back down Mount Whitney. We forged through

to Owens Lake not yet bone dry by then,
gypsum stalagmites on its saline flats
witnessing wetter winters, and two men
wiped off their brows, brushed off their cowboy hats.

Now the Sierras are so choked with snow,
so late in melting, cities far below
the Owens Valley, Vegas's neon glow,
shore up their waterworks for overflow.

Climate? We're just a nit on a gnat's ass.
Doubt me? Go buy a Mammoth Mountain Pass.

Desert Places, an Ode

Song for the Inyo

We park our Bronco way high above Bishop
to roam the White Mountains. The bristlecones
await us. Yesterday was a mishap,
seeking the Bodhisattva Merrell-Wolff
up Bishop Creek, tumbling down its gulf,
our goat track newly blocked by fallen stones.

Well before dawn we reached our parking place
too lofty for flowering alpine meadows
where the White Mountains soaring into space
corner the eldest grove of trees on earth,
five thousand years since blown seeds gave them birth.
They cast on the Sierras' skirts their shadows.

I feel no dearth of oxygen this day,
crackers, a California squirrel. Let's play.

King Clone

King Clone, twenty meters, creosote ring,
scientists think it twelve thousand years old.
Alan and I drove down to flee the cold
as the Mojave flowered into spring.

One organism like an aspen grove,
it made Abraham seem a suckling child,
no life on earth so weathered or so wild.
Under its sands some little lizards dove.

We had sought ancient living things before,
bristlecone pines, giant sequoia trees
growing on mountain summits or their knees,
flourishing near the California shore

thousands of years. King Clone makes them seem young.
Decades later a sonnet to be sung.

Grand Canyon

Muleback we started down Bright Angel Trail
    and lunched at Indian Wells
  on something more than peanut shells
    clutched with a muleteer's flail.

At last we reached the bridge to Hidden Ranch,
    deck under reconstruction,
  swaying above certain destruction
    to make the bravest blanch.

Ascending by a far more treacherous trail
    we rounded Skeleton Point,
  a cliff to make your courage fail,
    no Baptist to anoint

two postulants pelted by freakish snow.
    Bones of a lost mule train
  were bleached by desert sun and rain
    two thousand feet below.

The Drought of 1988

The summer sun bestows its benisons
on the Black Canyon's furtive denizens
    for half an hour a day.
Its sheer cliffs I like to describe as grey
    pre-Cambrian schist
no flat land acrophobe has ever kissed.

Before the Gunnison became a Park
    we came in pre-dawn dark,
scattering mule deer from the parking lot.
We'd never closed so nearly with them, not
    at Teddy Roosevelt Park
nor Utah where our national arches arc.

I crept up to the lip of that black cleft,
    my dizzying heart bereft.
Rate of fall, five times the Grand Canyon's speed,
that torrent snatched the breath of one in need
    of vertical relief
from a droughted-out, flat-broke farmer's grief.

Two Inventions

Silk inner stocking, raglan outer sock,
before Molefoam I limped on blistered feet.
Remove the boot, sit on a shattered rock
in the pine shadow of our night's retreat,

and take a sterile needle to my heel,
left and right toes that needed its attention,
then Band-Aids, a prick I could scarcely feel,
and shod again, pain I would never mention.

Then Molefoam, boots increased by half a size,
small patches, blister holes cut by Buck knife,
a bouldered, treeless summit as our prize,
sunscreen, two great inventions in my life.

The Great Yellowstone Fire

Elk and moose graze by the Lamar
winding through meadows to the Yellowstone.
We glass these massive beasts from our red car,
a Baby Benz. Pine forests, overgrown

and dying, the Great Drought of Eighty-eight,
are kindling over the slow rolling river
soon to force the mad flight from Silvergate.
In waves of heat the forests blur and quiver.

Pines must be harvested, that's their protection,
but take no chain saws to the banks of streams.
That trip through Yellowstone claims its own section,
the summer of my most dejected dreams,

crop failure, trying to walk a swaying wire.
Alan: "What this place needs is a good fire."

Vertical Relief

We fled our thirsty soil
to seek arduous toil,
giardia-free streams,
a tarn that land-locked gleams
under its montane wall
four hundred meters tall.
We shouldered heavy packs
as I did haversacks
when I was twelve years old.
We slept out in the cold,
waking in summer frost
to seek all we had lost.

We heard a Voice while summiting on stone:
It is not good for man to live alone.

Alan's Recruit

Mount of salvation, mountain of the Lord,
everywhere in the Bible, but for me
it was the cliffs, not God to be adored,
the tree lines gating on infinity.

Nature was to be worshipped. Alan too
lived for the wilds and lugged a heavy pack
to base camp, then summited for the view
much like a hunter on a Dall sheep's track.

Our first date was the Presidential Range,
fine crystal day, the blue Atlantic sheen
at line of sight. I did not find it strange
to skirt the snow of Tuckerman's Ravine.

I have praised many summits that I own.
Without Alan they would be all unknown.

Alan's Great Line for a Tee Shirt

For us every adventure was a quest,
        a new peak to be climbed,
        a sonnet to be rhymed
or salt water to sail from east to west.

The ten square miles of land that we acquired
        saddled with debt and woe,
        the house, the heavy snow
you shoveled till the winter you retired,

not yet ready to give up on the sea,
        whale roads where we were drawn
        half an hour before dawn
to flirt with reefs, courting mortality,

to dream we sailed beneath the cliffs of Dover:
Old sailors never die, they just keel over.

Monorhyme for Alan

I've cleaned a cock so my right hand is bloody.
Friend Alan, pray for your aging buddy.

I've tracked the floor because my boots are muddy.
Friend Alan, pray for your aging buddy.

I have a cold, my handkerchief is cruddy.
Friend Alan, pray for your aging buddy.

Sunburned, wind burned, my freckled face is ruddy.
Friend Alan, pray for your aging buddy.

Chucky is wiped out, snoring in his cuddy.
Friend Alan, pray for my little buddy.

Bible in hand, it's time for Tim to study.
Friend Alan, pray for your aging buddy.

The Cure

Your birth and death days barely a month apart,
our late May anniversary falls near.
Come summertime I have three days to clear
my calendar for matters of the heart,
but dates mean nothing. I converse in prayer
daily and dream of you on nights we pair.

I think I'll publish Alan's Ashes next.
"Feeney has more than I," you once complained.
Though our decades are hard to be explained,
the poems for you comprise a weighty text,
bulk of them written in the seven years
since your departure. Still the North Star steers

my feet by night over this snowy plain,
its bitter cold a sovereign cure for pain.

Easy Pickings

Air Feeney snatched an apple six feet high,
the ripe fruit dangling just above my eye
under the blue of a September sky.

Apples fermented, all our deer got drunk
as did the solitary midnight skunk,
and by late fall the fallen were all sunk

to mix with acorns as our orchard mast.
Come pick our apples, for they will not last.
Our picking poles could pluck the clinging fast

apples atop our seven hundred trees,
heap them in bags bulging at people's knees,
no more mosquitoes humming in the breeze.

Easy pickings and pies were on their way
two decades past, it seems just yesterday.

Isle Royale, First Trip

The Minong Ridge, a lake-level arête,
twenty-eight miles of grueling up and down,
a long ferry ride from Grand Portage town,
the skies wanted us miserable and wet.

The rain dripped through our tent, a Timberline
from REI, and soaked our sleeping bags,
the trip a shakedown for the rocky crags
we would assault so soon. The knotty pine

only I could ignite, a comfort zone
huddled just past our tent site. Shivering
we strapped on packs and no more quivering!
To kindle fire, sliver a jack pine cone,

moose and wolf, our interdependent quarry.
At mile sixteen, sodden, we took the ferry.

Square Top Plateau

The goat track to the high Square Top Plateau
stopped at a wall, small chimney choked with snow.
We had no rope but rock on either side,
so wedged our way upward to gain the wide
vista of the Wind Rivers' inner range,
all rock and ice, for us flatlanders strange
past grasping. Twenty-five and twenty-three,
we grew that day and found infinity
a two-day drive and two-day hike away.
Picturing that, it's time I kneel and pray.

Big Sandy Entrance

"One wolf alive, the sheep can never sleep,"
said the Basque shepherd to his Remington,
a lever action .30-30 gun.
His hatred for the predators ran deep,
black bears and wolves. Coyotes don't hunt so high,
too near the summit of Wyoming's sky.

We shared coffee beside his caravan
bonneted like our Conestoga wagons,
shared liquor and wine, exchanging flagons.
Herder, he could have come from Kazakhstan,
but overgrazing in the Pyrenees
led to these meadows high above the trees

in the Wind Rivers, a sacred haunt for two
flatlanders weary of their prairie view.

Bookends

Return to Mount Washington

Early Seventies and what were our odds
if only two percent of men are gays?
One in fifty, and yet our pagan gods
led us to plight our troth for all our days.

We climbed Mount Washington in our first week,
vertical mile from forest path to stone
Alan had sometimes summited alone,
but now he had his Eagle Scout to seek

the warming hut held down by logging chains
stapled to granite to withstand the gales,
strongest ever measured; my spirit sails
to that ascent, our blistered feet, their pains,

to Mount Katahdin in our farthest view,
to Alan twenty-four, Tim twenty-two.

Two Astronauts

My siblings bought Alan a telescope
        to view from our roof deck
        the moon's pockmarked wreck,
and patiently I taught him how to cope

with wheeled gizmos, equatorial mount,
        follow the trails of stars
        and the red orb of Mars,
Jupiter's moons, the three that we could count.

So we became sailors of stars and moon
        who often sailed the sea,
        yearned for infinity.
Neither perceived that he would leave so soon,

escape our planet's circuit of the sun
when I was fifty-nine, he sixty-one.

Out Far and In Deep

I dreamed we viewed the Very Large Array,
desert telescopes listening to the sky.
Strangers, do *you* observe *us* night and day,
this tiny planet where we laugh and cry?

We flew Virgin Galactic past the Hubble
probing the heights after its sell-by date,
a team of stargazers to keep its bubble
level, sailing the Heavens' tidal spate.

California, and up Mount Palomar
to see the largest mirror ever ground,
climbing switchbacks in Alan's rental car,
moonless, starry, windless without a sound,

to peer deeply back to the start of time,
another mountain we were meant to climb.

A Climb

Ira, second gravest of all my sins,
for when you to turn to wrath,
everyone loses, neither party wins,
the angry lose the path

leading their footsteps to the Rainbow Bridge,
my Alan's path to Heaven,
where an arête, a cruel saw-toothed ridge
trod when the eleven

Apostles, their apologist St. Paul,
scrambled in thinning air,
twenty-nine thousand feet that mountain wall,
antidote to despair

when all falls down and you are left to face
for one day more your poverty of grace.

In Memoriam

Like me Alan was wild for Charlie Beck.
    We took his woodcut book,
    gave it a probing look
and chose seven landscapes to stack the deck

of my first memoir, sent it off to press.
    Sunflowers green and gold
    in the first chapter sold
my editors, and so I told the mess

I'd made of farming, *Set the Ploughshare Deep*,
    a *prosimetrum*, verse
    with prose, a farmer's curse.
Charlie has passed beyond his well-earned sleep

to search new colors, surely a deeper hue
in Heaven than our flatland skies of blue.

Alan and Tim Beat a Retreat

Relief, aftermath of a mighty flood:
        strong kids get out of school
        to dike the drains that spool
through neighborhoods, their work boots caked with mud.

Our eight-armed Spiders stuff sand in the bags.
        Three colleges let out,
        farewell to years of drought.
Now students, shore up every wall that sags.

I well remember when we lost Grand Forks.
        Both fire and flood downtown,
        the Red rose up to drown
whole subdivisions, and we bobbed like corks

tossed by the freezing rain flung down from Heaven.
We were homeless, the Flood of Ninety-seven.

Kaleidoscopic Visitor

You never find the whiskey in my drawer
anymore. You are coming through the door
in dream, restored to your age twenty-four.

Or we backpack, climbing on switchback trails
on which our youthful ardor never fails
or I am helming, you are furling sails

on the blue sheet of Virgin Gorda Sound
bound for a mooring buoy, the mowed ground
of Bitter End. You pet a long dead hound

and bounce his bounding balls far down our lane.
I do my kernel counts on heading grain,
or double reefed, toss on the white-capped main.

Last night we slept beside a singing stream.
For thirty years I was too drunk to dream.

Another Sacrifice

Alan, another year
without you, and I fear
dying old and alone.
I am no heartless stone
but give money away
to hopeless drunks who stray
and pray to Dorothy Day.

I try to make things right,
beseeching you each night,
trying to work God's will.
Isaac climbs a high hill
while an archangel mourns
and I tangle my horns
in Old Testament thorns.

2016

More than three hundred pages in one year,
where did they come from? Many came from dreams,
decades of fording streams,
perhaps Polaris, star by which I steer.

The Alan poems are all grounded in loss,
verses of firm faith in the Holy Ghost,
the consecrated host,
both in the nights by which I spin and toss.

My five decades of hunting stand me well,
four Labradors serving so many years,
ashes scattered in tears,
safely arrived in Heaven, not in Hell.

Go romp with Alan in the asphodel.

Recurrent Dream of Heaven

I dream we will be twenty to twenty-five,
whatever is each person's physical peak,
masters of all we learned when we were alive
but have one less perplexity to seek
our answers to, no fear of mortality,
the Promise true, we have found infinity.

The earth will spin below like a movie reel,
and we'll look in to check on the young we love
struggling with their uncertainties, and I feel
in the great peanut gallery grouped above
we shall find all who preceded us in death,
and Bloody Mary will love Elizabeth.

Drinks on the house, and no one ever gets drunk,
my morning Mass is served by Father O'Shea,
the asphodel harbors no slavering skunk,
and my five beloved Labs join me in play,
pheasants, partridge, and doves drop to my gun
but rise to fly away. It is all in fun.

Alan awaits me, and they are not far,
the poets *lounging grandly* at Auden's bar.

The After Hunt

In dreams when I hunt in Heaven
Alan is always at choir.
Satan condemned to his fire,
we start promptly at seven.

Heaven has really no nights,
just midsummer twilight I've seen
near Hudson's Bay and the sheen
of the shimmering Northern Lights.

Hunters excused to skip Mass
form up by a blue-flowered field,
praying the cover will yield
birds that we shoot as they pass.

No mud, so nobody slogs
fielding our born-again dogs.

Last Prayer at Bedtime

I can't control where I will go in dream,
a mountain meadow or a coal field seam.
For chronic pain I take an opioid
that casts too many dreams into a void
where I forget them soon as I awake.
Alan, I dream *ars gratia artis*, stake
the claims of prosody into my sleep,
let my subconscious wander in a deep
region that I have never delved before,
my sailor makes his landfall on a shore
that never felt kisses of bows or keels.
I find new gravel underneath my wheels.
Come Holy Spirit, for You are the Lord
of every memory I have adored.

Matching my Becks

Soon I must match twelve Becks to nine new books
for a *Collected*. I have twenty-one,
for some, long decades of admiring looks.
The museum-grade photographs are done.

First book cover art? I said Early Snow.
    Alan selected seven
    for *Set the Ploughshare Deep*.
    Partnership made in heaven,
    I see Becks in my sleep,
especially when blizzards of winter blow

as they do now. Four volumes in a box,
more than a thousand pages it will run.
I wish Charlie had painted a red fox
leaving its den to greet this wintry sun.

Theocracy, 1973

I climbed Mount Helicon to meet Mnemosyne,
Mother of nine Muses
(I write as Chucky snoozes
three yards west of my knee.)
Euterpe is of course the Muse for me,
in charge of flutes and lyric poetry.

Paddling the gulf of Corinth in a coracle
to Delphi, I beseeched Apollo's Oracle,
sipped the Castilian Spring
and prayed for just one thing,
my pagan gods would make my verses lyrical.
I only knew the world was spherical,
but in my prairie fashion
I prayed with Murphy passion.

Well no, I also prayed Alan would wait for me.

Uffizi Palace, 1973

In the Uffizi there's a vast, bronze boar
bristling at Botticelli on the wall.
I fancy that he didn't grunt but roar
bursting from thickets to tear up the tall
bronzed spearmen, rip to shreds their baying hounds.
Death works both ways on the Greeks' killing grounds.

Primavera, The Birth of Venus, both
masterpieces of the High Renaissance.
Alan and I had just plighted our troth
when I flew off to Italy and France
thinking the Old World was a paradise
which Tim had to confirm with his young eyes.

Decades later, the Côte d'Azur in France,
Alan helmed our *Catana* out to dance.

Sous les Deux Pitons

A slow freighter spouted its diesel ash,
the sea flat calm, tropical sunset scene,
the only time I witnessed a green flash
and Alan had to tell me it was green.

So sheer the drop-off, rodes had scarcely scope,
our sterns lined to two palm trees on the shore,
big multihull chartered in certain hope
we'd buy our own, waiting just one year more.

Three hundred thousand, only one more debt,
paled compared to the millions on my land,
another little mountain to be met,
my finances careening out of hand.

My failed farm co-op so darkened my mind
red/green least of the things that struck me blind.

The Drake Passage

I.
A supertanker bore down on our port,
    the white bone at its nose
    heading for Heaven knows
under the ruins of a British fort
    built by Sir Francis Drake
to claim these islands for his sovereign's sake.

Then suddenly a hundred feet of chain
    shackled onto our plow
    cascaded from our prow.
Our anchor pin had failed us once again.
    The ship seemed standing still,
big as a British Virgin Island hill,

but it was steaming nearly twenty knots,
a fearsome threat to fragile sailing yachts.
    Windlass quick as you can,
fire off a flare. Radio Pan Pan Pan.

II.
The Christmas Winds could shut us in for days.
    We didn't want to fight
    the seas to Norman Bight.
Cerulean blue skies, not a hint of haze,

but there were elephants on the horizon,
    sunshine-refracted waves
    dancing on sailors' graves,
to us Dakotans herds of charging bison.

III.

A mile southwest we saw the plume of smoke,
        too far away to glass.
        Never, ever burn gas,
a smoking boat is not a harmless joke.

We raced downwind to render our assistance,
        but suddenly a boom
        swept us as if a broom
swept clear the Drake Passage with its insistence.

Leaky fuel line, a frayed electric wire
        make an impressive bomb.
        They swam with some aplomb,
fortunate victims of that engine fire.

A boat blazing under the tropic sun?
Headsail and main, fling wing on wing and run!

Roller Furler

Our boat a thirty-eight foot Beneteau,
its roller furler snarled near Jost van Dyck,
so we limped back, our main reefed for the blow,
ungainly as a smashed-up boyhood bike,
our headsail lashed around the forward stay,
and anchored off a reef-protected beach.
We rowed ashore for glasses of Mount Gay.
The BVIs had many truths to teach.

Moorings sent us its little service truck,
a skilled shipwright and a replacement line,
then off to Virgin Gorda, better luck.
Snug in our V-berth sailors could entwine
solidly anchored in their evening ease,
waiting the morrow and a Christmas breeze.

Hurricane Haul-out

Wilma knocked our *Dreamweaver* off its blocks,
its topmast nestled in our neighbor's shrouds,
no more damage than were it kissed by clouds,
its keel scratched by the gravel and the rocks.

In Florida's fourth hurricane that year,
a Cat 1, Wilma veered from west to east,
of four storms its ferocity the least.
Safety lay up a river five miles near

and haul-out at the yard where we first launched,
where I tried to ride the outgoing tide,
so used to my twin diesels side by side,
the flood of memory I've never staunched,

the shame of torque overruling my wheel
and tide whirlpooling round my clueless keel.

Rage Sea, an Ode

Departing Miami

We loved rough weather and we loved wild waves.
    What is a lifeline for
    or a latched cabin door?
Show me the whirlpools when a rage sea raves,

and landbound I will take it under sail
    or outbound under power.
    You cannot choose your hour,
long trips to make, seas burying your rail.

Alan would go below in a rage sea
    wearing his orange life vest,
    a strobe light on his chest,
Government Cut a short-lived misery,

a Coast Guard ensign blaring his bull horn.
Try it, I guarantee you'll be reborn.

January Landfall

Candy-striped stacks over Port Everglades:
        an egret by the beach
        spears every fish in reach.
We marvel at how hungrily he wades.

We have sailed in powered by jib alone,
        rip tide and a rage sea,
        love, only you and me,
threading two massive jetties made of stone.

Now it is time to winch the furling line,
        fire up the engines, two
        small Yanmars, time for you
to take our helm. The Christmas wind was fine,

and we were blown to heaven, fifty miles
north of Miami, our faces creased with smiles.

Rage Sea

Marry the full flow of outgoing tide
        with a gale blown onshore,
we are in for a roller coaster ride,
set storm sail, and ignore the breakers' roar.

But outbound it is a tooth-cracking trip,
        mark the small craft warning
unless you care not for the hours-long drip
from sodden sea togs ruining your morning.

Love, you and I have hazarded five times
        the risks of a rage sea,
three in, two out, and now I harvest rhymes
owed to our mad, youthful temerity.

No more sailing, no more rage seas for me.

First Mate and Skipper

A compass rose lies hidden in my head.
    That's why I'm never lost
    though often detours cost
time on a road not taken which has led

to new gravel, seeking a new horizon.
    Born for dead reckoning,
    the untried beckoning,
my north-south sense true as a herd of bison.

It is a gift most useful out at sea.
    Oh, we had GPS
    and charts, and we'd say yes
to auto-helm spelling my love and me

on wild traverses up the Francis Drake
or down the Keys, routes we would undertake
for novelty and high adventure's sake.

M.V. Fugle

We never motored south to Hampton Roads.
    Stefan and Alan did,
    but there they were forbid
passage. A submarine with nuclear loads

steamed forth to start six months beneath the sea.
    She was Poseidon Class,
    her boys had balls of brass
and more than young Murphy's temerity.

Thirty ICBMs under their lids,
    ninety torpedoes, who
    would challenge such a crew
even though half of them were beardless kids?

Our final boat, Alan would sail no more.
    She hosted Irish priests
    for fiery curry feasts
but never fared far out of sight from shore.

Fugle was sold, and for New England bound
our portly Main ship promptly ran aground.

Tiny Chantey

Heads'l, stays'l, mains'l, mizzen,
trim long enough your beard will wizen.

Tell tales, wind vane, compass, leach cord,
misread, your ship is gripped with discord.

Length overall, mast height and beam,
figures that visit you in dream.

Halyard, jibsheet, mainsheet, downhaul,
winch long enough they'll be your downfall.

Sea Legs

After a week at sea
you step onto dry land
and feel it heave beneath you.

Go swim in the sea
whatever you have planned,
and let the seaweed wreathe you.

This is the legacy
your captain and deck hand
take time to bequeath you.

Sink your toes in the sand.

Three Days in June 2001

"I've always thought the Yankees had something to do with it."
—General George Pickett explaining the slaughter

Pitching their tents with wooden mallets
the Blue and Gray camped face to face
to settle things with bullets (not with ballots)
for lasting glory or disgrace.
On the third day Pickett's Charge
carved in our nation's history so large,
settled the Union in a flood
of carcasses floating in their own blood.

One time in Pennsylvania
we walked both Gettysburg and Valley Forge
to contemplate the cold, convulsive mania
riving our world. The Delaware's ancient gorge
gentles its way to Chesapeake Bay
where we'd make sail well before break of day
with Alan at the helm,
half sweet, half salt that watery realm.

There we imagined Lincoln on his train
going to Gettysburg to teach
grief in his brief great speech.
We raised at dawn our first self-reefing main,
and Hecht's new verses we would kill to write
kept us awake most of the following night.

For you the two are alike:
the darkness and the light.

See "Lux et Tenebrae" in *Mortal Stakes* (Murphy 29).
The final couplet is from the Sullivan translation of Psalm 139.

Return to *S.V. Arabella*

Arabella, our sleekest, fastest ship
  booked for a four-day trip,
lay at anchor with Providence in view.
Working deck forbidden to all but crew,
but one look and the savvy skipper knew
the two of us were serious sailors too,
  so Alan took the helm.
Three matched masts tall as a Fargo elm,
  three headsails and three mains,
giant anchors windlassed on massive chains,
  we set forth at ten knots,
stiff breeze, our wake rocking the smaller yachts.

Her sails so tall they could claw wind from clouds,
  wrist-thick its stays and shrouds,
  salons outside and in,
she punched thirty degrees from the breeze's chin
  bound for Nantucket Bay
  ground tackle under weigh.
Two twelve meters that won America's Cup
bobbed at their buoys as we were winching up.

  Tiny our bunks, short beds,
  passageway showers and heads,
schooner twenty-six feet from beam to beam
  boarded last night in dream,
one hundred sixty feet from stem to stern.
Wake before dawn to watch the sunrise burn
  through the light fog or haze,
  the evenings of our days
touring the island churches, back to sea,
Alan face to face with mortality,
prescient departure from the paths of men.
We never sailed, never made love again.

Wintry Gratitude, an Ode

Seven Good Fridays Later

First *Triduum*, the Long Gospel of John,
you said you'd never heard me read that well,
fourteen minutes, the church under John's spell,
the horror that prefigures Easter dawn.

Cloaked in purple the crucifix of Christ,
next night the Vigil, candles in the dark,
then daybreak and the Gospel of St. Mark.
The clothes for which the Roman soldiers diced

cast off, the risen Lord in radiant white,
the rock rolled from the tomb, angel on guard.
Dear friend, I know your last five years were hard,
your Temple curtain torn in two each night,

but you lived to embrace Christ's revelation
from the *Via Dolorosa's* final station.

Solemn Mass for the Dead

With *Dona eis requiem* we end
    the *Agnus Dei* as we pray
the *Missa pro defunctis* for a friend
    who spent decades astray,
    a solemn way to spend
Timor mortis on a funereal day,

a day to wear my darkest chalk-striped suit
    and polished wing-tipped shoes,
black vestments for the celebrants. A flute
    joins in the *Kyrie*,
and every candle in the church is a lit fuse
to blow our daily certitudes away.

Ave atque vale, Hail and farewell,
Catullus called after his brother fell.

All Soul's Night

"All Souls' Night," my favorite poem by Yeats,
spoken from memory once more last night
when Christ as every night casts down the Gates
of Hell to lead His people to the light:

five celebrants, all their silk vestments black
one day a year, save Masses for the Dead
where the departed seek their upward track.
Now seven years after our Savior led

Alan homeward to claim his last reward
for turning David's Psalms to English verse,
the Rainbow Bridge guarded by Michael's sword,
my loved translator trying to reimburse

our Savior for his final agony,
I offer Mass in Alan's memory.

Prayer to Alan

Now I live modestly, much like a monk
who sought no monastery when you died,
my gravest sin *Superbia*, the pride
taken in poetry. Now never drunk
I take dictation from the Holy Spirit,
go to confession and my daily Mass,
prayerfully hunt my puppy's prairie grass,
the high bar to salvation? Hope I clear it,
my summons home, pray that I daily hear it.

My dearest earthly comfort is my friends,
devoted few who fear how I grow fragile
unlike that boy bedded when I was agile,
tirelessly trekking to the mountains' ends.
I trust you hear this prayer your lover sends.

Wintry Gratitude

Modest my martyrdom for poetry,
        no slow roast on a spit,
        only the play of wit
with metaphor, music, and memory.

I hope to die singing two kinds of praise,
        the world by which I'm awed,
        the majesty of God,
both of which carry Murphy through his days.

The pole star of my soul is gratitude
        for my deferring death,
        drawing each day the breath
of cold in this high northern latitude.

Thanks too, All-Father, for the friend you gave
with whom I'll reunite beyond the grave.

Fiftieth Anniversary

It's fifty years since my unlikely dream
to follow Robert Frost and William Yeats,
to storm Mount Helicon, the Muses' Gates.
Slowly my trickles turned into a stream.

Much of great import happened to me young,
the sexuality I realized,
the thirty thousand lines I memorized,
the classical guitar I left unstrung.

Most of all Alan who allayed my fears,
who shored up my confidence in my art,
partnership of the brain and of the heart
that somehow lasted thirty-seven years
until alas, his slow death did us part.
Seven years later now I shed no tears.

Seventh Anniversary, an Ode

I.

A month from now it will be seven years
since Alan "shuffled off this mortal coil,"
no more translations, no more frenzied toil,
a terminus to cancer and its fears.

Still here on earth, I'm toiling every day.
After a long break I turned sixty-five,
took up my pen, proof I am still alive,
and love, my head has shed all trace of grey.

Lonely of course, deprived of the true friend
the Holy Spirit destined for my lips.
Thinner and bonier grow my slim hips,
and Daily Mass equips me for my end,

for our reunion where mortality
is a mere foothill from infinity.

II.

After four decades of our brotherhood
            I have my prayer,
deep dreams in which I climb my winding stair,
            days bad and good,

but I plod on, seven years since you died.
            I'm faring well,
having long since cast off my grieving shell
            each day I've tried

to live as you would wish, a long, swift life
            written in stars
and the slow, solar circuitry of Mars,
            honing my knife

to slash off the unworthy from my soul.
Clasped in each other's arms some nights we roll.

III.
Lay me doun love, o lay me low,
and say your fervent prayers again,
whispering softly when you go
Surely he was an honest man.

Burn my corpse. Spread my grey ashes
on your dear grave, let say a Mass,
dip fingers where the water splashes
its holy font after I pass.

Truth be told I'm growing weary,
and the trail I tread is lonely.
Oftentimes my dreams are eerie
with prefigurement, for only

in death shall we lie united,
our fast promises requited.

IV.

We swore "Till death do us part."
It did some seven years ago.
I hold him closely in my heart,
he prays for Timothy below.
I thought his editing my art
would be his legacy, but no,
I have decades of memories
revolving as I hunt these leafless trees.

I shared his passion for the sea
I've not sailed for many a year,
for the full moon at perigee,
for the North Star by which I steer
and mountainous geology,
his canvas where the aeons are brushed clear.
From me he learned true love of poetry.

Lastly the great thing that we share,
the faith we found so near his end,
Faeder ure, our Savior's prayer
which heavenward at Mass we send
preceded by the words "We dare
to say." Pray it for me, dear friend.

Hiking All Night, an Ode

Mount Rearguard

We drove a 4X4 new Audi 80,
and neither we nor our backpacks were weighty,
but Alan had to roll rocks off the tall
cliff faces carved into a plateau's wall
to reach trailhead. Then a long, level walk
to Sliderock Lake, grassy, scarcely a rock.

Then Alan climbed Mount Rearguard's lower slopes
whose scree defeated him, his boyish hopes
of peering deeper into the Beartooth Range.
I fished for brookies, fruitless for a change,
for the lake, nearly icebound, held no fish
wakeful enough to grab a flying wish.

Next day we packed out, each bearing his load,
and giant slalomed down Hellroaring Road.

West Rosebud Entrance

I fished a folding bucksaw from my pack
and felled two slender aspens for a bridge
to cross a stream which roared, on the attack
with snowmelt from a sheared-off Beartooth ridge

high on our left, the Froze to Death Plateau.
We loved that name and would have made that climb,
but it was June, the trail too deep in snow,
so on to Island Lake. Another time,

but that time never came. For thirty years
ranging the Wyoming-Montana line
we trekked or packed on horses. Greenhorn fears
gave way to trust whatever the incline

as horses hauled us when we grew too old
to hump our gear up to the snow and cold.

Sunlight Basin Pass

We glimpsed Cloud Peak from Sunlight Basin Pass!
    the air so clear, a feast
    for Eagles to our east
hunting above two hundred miles of grass

dividing trekkers from the Bighorn Range
    we'd skirt on our return
    with no more heart to burn.
Each journey to Wyoming marked a change,

for you a birthday, me another year
    trying to stay afloat,
    buy you another boat.
To Red Lodge in another Ford we'd steer

to wind the switchbacks up to Beartooth Pass
and fish its tarns. Christ polishes their glass.

Alan's Ranges

Batholiths upthrust from their ancient sea,
the shattered sandstones clinging to their shoulders,
        the jumbled summit boulders
for young rock hoppers such as you and me,

drew us in youth, yearning forever west
to flee our graveled grandeur, the Great Plains,
        shucking my farmer's chains,
to put our boots and backpacks to the test.

Cascades, so young they seemed but cinder cones.
Back to the granites of the Great Divide
        and ponies we would ride
to catch an earful from the pedal tones

of God's creation, the retreating shore
where the uplifting peaks within us soar.

Dream Before Dawn

Alan, we're still switchbacking up one peak,
dusty our boots, treeless the camp we seek,
rocks where the pikas scream their screeching squeak.

You have made your summit ahead of me
as usual, krumholtz, the knee high tree
on which we pitch our packs. What do you see?

I think you see what I glimpse far below
on the high prairie where the blizzards blow
and bury my brother farmers deep in snow.

Looking aloft you see a sky we'll make
black as the course which I will overtake,
obsidian my steel has yet to flake,

the black that terrifies you as a child
and then exalts you when you're growing wild.

Hiking All Night

Alan, last night we hiked a forest road
under construction. There a stark massif
soared in the wintry air. Trivial load
our daypacks, surely three miles of relief,

so this was no trail we had hiked before,
no trail on earth of which this hiker knows,
tree line our goal, where pines break on a shore
of rock upthrust into the realm of snows

we reached, cramponed, with ropes that I could splice.
We broke for lunch beside a gurgling stream
green with the flour of granite ground by ice,
a jasmine tea discolored by no cream.

Our waking world not always what it seems,
I love it when you come to me in dreams.

Upper and Lower Tree Lines

Tree belts grow narrower when we set forth
to climb ranges farther and farther north
from xeric basins to the rock and snow
where only crazed backpackers care to go,
pikas, marmots, ravens, and mountain goats,
none of them fattened on our flatland oats.

Far in the North there are no trees at all,
ranges unforested, each stony wall
soaring above the tundra and the sea,
and there sometimes I dream of you and me
carrying canteens to a modest peak
where an expansive view is all we seek,

where I am twenty-two, you twenty-four,
eight long degrees north of a forest floor.

Epode

Four months, four dreams, all set at altitude
you longed to reach, born by the Hudson River.
Westward fifty degrees of longitude,
layered in woolens so we wouldn't shiver

above ten thousand feet on mountain meadows
blossoming wildly in their three week season,
no lodgepole pines to cast their fragrant shadows,
our urge to climb a most unearthly reason

for such exertions, that and the dusty prairie
we left behind, the drought, the debt, the anger,
all for our scrambles where the pitch was scary,
campfires occasion for exhausted languor.

Old friend, give my regards to our Redeemer.
I'm studying to be an expert dreamer.

Epilogue: Long Regret

Alan, today I start another year
widowed, and this year brings the count to eight.
I have confounded, love, your long-held fear
death by whiskey would be my brutish fate.
I fear, however, that you might be appalled
to see me stuck here, so utterly walled

without you. Here I'm mining memories
from realms you drove me to I'd never seen,
our switchback trails to tree line's dwarfish trees
and the dawn's glassy, blue Caribbean sheen,
the day's first cat's paws, promising our wind.
Stricken in conscience by one way I sinned,

the crime that I am most penitent of,
buried in debt and shackled to the plough?
My failures to articulate my love.
Let this volume be my repentant vow.

—1 January 2018

Glossary, Attributions, and Musings

FC, American Kennel Club Field Champion; NFC, National Field Champion.

Caveant Lepusculi: Little rabbits beware.

"Predator, an Ode:" The first line in "Two Hunters" is lifted from Netflix's "The Hunt." All poems in the ode were similarly inspired by this gripping series narrated by Attenborough.

"Second Sinfonietta" is published in *Deed of Gift.*

Lars Herseth's father, Ralph, was instrumental in the creation of the Sand Lake and adjacent James River National Wild Life Refuges, critical staging grounds for the Central Flyway, where I have been royally entertained for fifty years.

"Section Seventeen": *Sowing their hated seeds* comes from "Salsola Kali," published in *Mortal Stakes.* "Heartbeat of the Hunt" is from "Rhymes for the Rosebud," published in *Hunter's Log.*

"Wandering the Land with a Mind Swathed in Wool" is the opening sonnet in *Intimations of Mortality* by William Wordsworth.

In "Tracking the Cocks," the italicized couplet comes from two earlier hunting poems, "Long Shot" and "i.m. Elmwood's Bold Fenian."

"Air Labrador" in my "Ode to November" describes Feeney's greatest retrieve, witnessed by Steve Syrdal.

"*Address to the Deil*" is Burns's title, "Devil in Lallans Scots."

"*Ad altare dei,*" translates "to the altar of God" in the Latin Mass and is also the Boy Scouts' high honor for Catholic kids.

Return to China: *Thinking of happiness, I think of that.* See Richard Wilbur's "Running," the great "Pindaric Ode," which has so influenced me for nearly fifty years. That line is the end of Dick's strophe. The Yellow Hat *Gelugpa* is the Dalai Lama's school, and this is my favorite visualization meditation. Kuan Yin, goddess of mercy, is traditionally painted as riding atop a swan.

Scop (poet in Anglo Saxon): *Wyrd* and *dom* both translate as fate. Weird and doom have ancient baggage. The epigraph is the last line of Beowulf's death scene, which we translated as "And his soul sought the doom of the truthful."

"*deal us a last, hard blow.*" See Wilbur's "A Storm in April," a model to me for decades.

Unlicensed: Cessna 185s appear in several poems, the only plane I ever really flew.

I gave Dick Wilbur Leslie Monsour's first book and read him her "Burrowing Bees" in Cummington, to his great delight.

4 July: NRO is *National Review Online*.

"Thysells, an Ode": Staunch: 1) watertight, 2) strongly built, 3) loyal in character.

"Green, a Double Sonnet": The epigraph is from my poem "Patience."

Wheat: "Go home boy . . ." is Robert Penn Warren's directive to me when I was twenty-one, verbatim.

Amor pro patria: love of country. *Sic transit gloria mundi:* So passes the glory of the world. Dick Wilbur is the last of my friends who served in WW II. Victor Davis Hanson, classicist and military historian, published his great essay on Pericles and Lincoln on Memorial Day 2017.

The first line of "Alan's Recruit" is a found pentameter in a sermon by Fr. Mitch Pacwa, S.J.

"Byron lounging grandly at the bar" is a line from Auden's *Letter from Iceland*.

“Early Spring” was published by *Chronicles*. When my publishers catch up with me, all twenty-three of my Charlie Beck woodcuts will have appeared on or in my books. I fell in love with his work at age twelve, and ours has been a great partnership. He was still doing fine work when he died at ninety-four.

Commonweal published “Alan’s Ranges, Dream Before Dawn,” “Hiking All Night, Upper and Lower Treeline,” and “Epode, all from Hiking All Night,” the concluding sonnet sequence of this collection. My editor, Matthew Boudway, also published “Letter to Belmont” and one of the three major odes for Allan, “Wintry Gratitude.”

Think published “Prayer for my Sixty-seventh Pentecost” and “Sonnet at Midnight.”

First Things published “January 25, an Ode.”

Gray’s Sporting Journal published “Ode to the Sharptails,” and my editor, Russ Lumpkin, has “Three Mile Sonnet,” “Ralph Herseth,” and “St. Lucy’s Day” in his hold file, all of them ambitious odes.

Presence published “*God Does Not Play Dice.*”

The Hudson Review published “The Seekers and Strength to Change” from “Ode to China.”

Able Muse published “Bound for Beulah” and “Three Loves in Autumn.”

About the Author

Timothy Iver Murphy of Fargo, North Dakota, passed away in his home on Saturday, June 30, 2018, at the age of sixty-seven. He was born in Hibbing, Minnesota, on January 10, 1951. Raised in Moorhead, Minnesota, he was active in high school speech and debate and graduated from Moorhead High School in 1968 as president of his senior class. Tim was an Eagle Scout and member of the Order of the Arrow. He worked summers at Camp Wilderness near Park Rapids, Minnesota, as a Scout craft aide and a commissioner.

Tim attended Yale University, pursuing his interest in poetry and undertaking a tutorial with Robert Penn Warren. He was named Scholar of the House in Poetry, and he graduated from Yale with a BA in 1972. Tim joined his father in the life insurance, pension, and estate planning business, V.R. Murphy and Sons, Inc., winning numerous national sales awards. His entrepreneurial interests led to his raising equity capital for partnerships in a number of local companies: Timco Farms, Bell Farms, Orchard Glen Development, DakTech, and Bytespeed LLC.

Tim loved hiking, sailing, farming, and hunting with his black Labs. All were inspiration for his poetry, which was his great passion in life. A fascinating and complicated man, he wrote deceptively simple poetry exploring universal themes: faith, family, spirituality, death, farming, friendship. His work is rooted in place: the Red River of the North, North Dakota, and the Great Plains.

His poetry is published in prominent journals including *Poetry*, *Quadrant*, *Hudson Review*, *New Criterion*, *Chronicles*, *Alabama Literary Review*, and *Gray's Sporting Journal.* His books include *The Deed of the Gift* (Story Line Press 1998), *Set the Ploughshare Deep* (Ohio University Press 2002), *Mortal Stakes and Faint Thunder* (Dakota Institute Press 2011), *Hunter's Log* (Dakota Institute Press 2011), *Devotions* (North Dakota State University Press 2017), and *Hunter's Log: Volumes II & III* (North Dakota State University Press 2019). Tim collaborated with his long-time partner Alan Sullivan on a translation of *Beowulf* (Longman 2004).

About the Press

North Dakota State University Press (NDSU Press) exists to stimulate and coordinate interdisciplinary regional scholarship. These regions include the Red River Valley, the state of North Dakota, the plains of North America (comprising both the Great Plains of the United States and the prairies of Canada), and comparable regions of other continents. We publish peer reviewed regional scholarship shaped by national and international events and comparative studies.

Neither topic nor discipline limits the scope of NDSU Press publications. We consider manuscripts in any field of learning. We define our scope, however, by a regional focus in accord with the press's mission. Generally, works published by NDSU Press address regional life directly, as the subject of study. Such works contribute to scholarly knowledge of region (that is, discovery of new knowledge) or to public consciousness of region (that is, dissemination of information or interpretation of regional experience). Where regions abroad are treated, either for comparison or because of ties to those North American regions of primary concern to the press, the linkages are made plain. For nearly three-quarters of a century, NDSU Press has published substantial trade books, but the line of publications is not limited to that genre. We also publish textbooks (at any level), reference books, anthologies, reprints, papers, proceedings, and monographs. The press also considers works of poetry or fiction, provided they are established regional classics or they promise to assume landmark or reference status for the region. We select biographical or autobiographical works carefully for their prospective contribution to regional knowledge and culture. All publications, in whatever genre, are of such quality and substance as to embellish the imprint of NDSU Press.

Our name changed to North Dakota State University Press in January 2016. Prior to that, and since 1950, we published as the North Dakota Institute for Regional Studies Press. We continue to operate under the umbrella of the North Dakota Institute for Regional Studies, located at North Dakota State University.

Index of Titles and First Lines